Where Are the Women Architects?

Where Are the Women Architects?
Despina Stratigakos

Published by Princeton University Press
Princeton and Oxford
in association with Places Journal

Princeton University Press, 41 William Street, Princeton, New Jersey 08540
In the United Kingdom: Princeton University Press, 6 Oxford Street,
Woodstock, Oxfordshire OX20 1TW
press.princeton.edu

Cover illustration: Denise Scott Brown, photograph by Robert Venturi.
Courtesy of Venturi, Scott Brown and Associates, Inc.

Library of Congress Cataloging-in-Publication Data
Stratigakos, Despina, author.
Where are the women architects? / Despina Stratigakos.
pages cm
Includes bibliographical references and index.
ISBN 978-0-691-17013-8 (pbk. : alk. paper) 1. Women architects. I. Title.
NA1997.S77 2016
720.82—dc23
2015027345
British Library Cataloging-in-Publication Data is available

Designed and composed by Yve Ludwig in Akkurat and Mercury
Printed on acid-free paper
Printed in China
10 9 8 7 6 5 4 3 2 1

To my grandmothers

One sold her dowry to study and become a teacher;
the other, forbidden any education as a girl, sat on the
school steps and wept

Acknowledgments

This book has been inspired by conversations and collaborations over the years with women who believed that architecture must change and decided to do something about it. The late Milka Bliznakov, who founded the International Archive of Women in Architecture at Virginia Tech, and on whose advisory committee I once served, demonstrated the passion and care involved in preserving the historical record. Beverly Willis, founder of the Beverly Willis Architecture Foundation (BWAF) in New York City, has been a model for bringing a broad variety of people to the table through participatory public education and synergistic partnerships with academia and industry; I am honored to serve on the BWAF board of trustees. At the Royal Institute of Technology in Stockholm, Meike Schalk and Katja Grillner, co-founders of the feminist architecture and research collective FATALE, have included me in their conversations about pedagogy and social outreach, providing insights from an international perspective. I have also benefited from the generosity of researchers in other countries who have undertaken major studies of gender equity in architecture and shared their experiences with me, including Annmarie Adams at McGill University and Karen Burns and Justine Clark at the University of Melbourne. Closer to home, I have talked shop and strategized with Lori Brown of Syracuse University, who co-founded ArchiteXX to create mentoring networks and programs to help young women stay in architectural practice. At the University at Buffalo, Kelly Hayes McAlonie, my collaborator on Architect Barbie, spurs us both on in the search for novel ways to raise women architects' visibility. These women, and many others not mentioned here, have been my village in the shared goal of reforming architecture, and I thank them all for their ideas, energy, and good company.

Equally important to shaping this book have been my many conversations about architecture and publishing with Nancy Levinson, editor and executive director of *Places Journal*. She encouraged me to explore the possibilities of online publishing, and two of the chapters included here, on Architect Barbie and on Wikipedia, began as *Places* articles. I am deeply grateful for her thoughtful engagement with my work and to Josh Wallaert, senior editor, for his contributions. At Princeton University Press, I offer special thanks to my editor, Michelle Komie, for her vision and support. This is the second book on which we have collaborated, and I know we are not done yet. My thanks also go to Marilyn Martin, an exceptional copyeditor.

Two anonymous readers commented on the manuscript, and I am grateful for their valuable suggestions. The chapter on Architect Barbie owes a particular debt to the architecture faculty and students at the University of Michigan, who, years before she became a real toy, gamely agreed to try their hand at designing prototypes. Their dolls continue to be a source of provocation and amusement. I had the good fortune to write this book while teaching a graduate seminar on gender and architecture at the University at Buffalo School of Architecture and Planning. Over the semester, the participants, an incredible group of young women, nourished and challenged my writing with their observations and questions. I thank them for reminding me what this is all about.

Where Are the Women Architects?

Where Are the Women Architects?

Walking into a lecture hall, attending a convention, sitting in a boardroom, participating on a jury, or strolling through an exhibition—these are just some of the times that I have wondered, "Where are the women architects?" And I am not alone in asking this question. In the past few years, a chorus of voices has begun to ask why women, who first began studying architecture 140 years ago, continue to struggle to gain a foothold in the profession. Despite women's increasing enrollments in architecture schools since the 1980s, their numbers in practice have flatlined, and the higher one moves up the career ladder, the further they decline. At the top, measured by the profession's highest awards and honors, they drop to nearly zero. This attrition of women in architecture and the career hurdles they face readily evoke building metaphors, such as a leaky pipeline and the glass ceiling. When one considers, however, the generations of dreams and work and ambitions that have been lost to us, it seems that the more appropriate term for this phenomenon is tragedy.

In this book I set out to explore a question that has long troubled the profession, diminishes its luster, and shows no sign of fading away. I begin in chapter 1 with a history of the question and its contexts, stretching from the 1870s to the 1970s. Since the nineteenth century, women as well as men have posed the question of women's absence in architecture, some arguing for change and others for the status quo. My aim here is less to chronicle women's entry into the profession, which other authors and books have done, than to track an unfinished dialogue that has haunted architecture—in a cycle of acknowledging and then abandoning its gender issues—for a very long time.

Chapter 2 brings the picture up to date, looking at the current status of women in architecture, from their first experiences as students to their climb up the professional ladder. The view that emerges makes clear why the question of women's slow progress has reemerged in recent years, and more urgently than ever: it is hard to look at the statistics and not feel alarmed. Female architecture graduates continue to struggle to enter and stay in practice, large salary gaps persist, sexism on the job seems to be getting worse, and women remain vastly underrepresented in the profession's leadership roles. Indeed, this perspective suggests less the question of why women leave architecture than of why they would pursue it at all.

But if we look at the status of the question itself—how it is being pushed in unprecedented ways and by a new range of voices into the forefront of public and professional discussions about gender equity—the sense of a hopeless and grim continuity begins to dissolve. Indeed, this book has been timed to help identify and strengthen a rising third wave of feminism in architecture, which follows on the first wave that emerged at the end of the nineteenth century and the second wave that began in the early 1970s and continued into the 1990s. The current movement is not entirely distinct from the second one; many of the participants are the same, and their voices did not, in any case, disappear in the interim. What marks it, however, as a new and exciting development are the many young women (and men) who are joining in the call for change, as well as the international reach of their interventions. This new generation of advocates harness today's conditions and possibilities, including global marketing and new forms of technology and communication.

Mattel's creation and launch of Architect Barbie in 2011 spawned a global reaction that exposed, for the first time, just how effective social media could be in catalyzing discontent with the gendered status quo in architecture. In the discussions about and around this new Barbie, explored in chapter 3, her critics and supporters delved into the conditions facing women in architecture, revealing a shared desire for change but differing viewpoints among older and younger generations on how to achieve it. The doll also brought to the fore the issue of missing role models, in terms of both real women within the profession and their lack of representation in the broader popular culture. Although any number of television shows, movies, or novels present us with strong female characters who are doctors or lawyers, female characters who are architects are hard to find.

The absence of women is also keenly felt in the world of architecture prizes, and chapter 4 addresses why women architects are so rarely sighted on the podium when the profession bestows it most coveted awards. The chapter begins with a look at how the architectural press reacted when Zaha Hadid broke the glass ceiling of the Pritzker Architecture Prize in 2004. The coverage revealed that the bias against women as innovative creators, already expressed in the nineteenth century and explored in chapter 1, never fully went away. This was certainly not news to Denise Scott Brown, who, in 1991, was passed over for the Pritzker Architecture Prize that was awarded solely to her design partner and husband, Robert Venturi, in part for their joint work. The chapter concludes by exploring how, in 2013, two Harvard architecture students, representative of a younger feminist generation and its political uses of new communication networks, launched a petition on Change.org to demand belated recognition for Scott Brown. The petition, which to date has garnered nearly twenty thousand signatures globally, rocked the architectural world, even if it did not succeed in its mission to convince the Pritzker Architecture Prize committee to set the record straight.

Although the Scott Brown petition harnessed the power of the Internet to raise awareness globally about how critics and juries have overlooked women architects in the past, digital technologies are not in themselves a solution. The erasure of women architects from the historical record and the lack of information and public awareness about their work will not improve in the digital age unless more women in architecture actively engage with the new information and communication technologies to ensure their own visibility. Chapter 5 continues the exploration of gender equity in architecture and digital activism through the lens of Wikipedia. Recent feminist criticism of Wikipedia has brought attention to how male editors' bias against entries on women has served to erase or marginalize their presence from the world's most frequently used reference source. Women architects, as it turns out, are also not immune to the editors' deleting proclivities. I consider the reasons for women architects' absence on Wikipedia and why we should care about this website and others like it.

The rise of a third wave of feminism in architecture has, unsurprisingly, provoked a counterreaction. Insisting on architecture's essential meritocracy, opponents of change, who also deploy the power of social media, argue that gender does not matter and that talent alone should determine who succeeds. They fail to acknowledge, however, that the profession's unfriendly climate for women already eliminates a large and vital part of that talent pool. And that means more mediocre architecture, however you cut it.

In this book I hope to provide insights, sometimes from unusual vantage points, into the challenges that the architectural profession faces at a critical juncture in its history in addressing and righting a long legacy of discrimination against women. It is also meant as a clarion call. For those of you who, like me, care deeply about architecture and want to see it become a truly inclusive profession, I ask that you be vocal and make trouble.

Chapter 1

May Women Practice Architecture? The First Century of Debate

The question of women's absence from architecture has a surprisingly long history. In July 1872, women's rights advocate Julia Ward Howe gave a lecture on women artists to the Victorian Discussion Society in London. She wondered why architecture had no female practitioners, given what she saw as their aptitude for the field and potential contributions. "An architect ought to have taste," she reasoned. "Women ought to agitate to be articled to some of our architects, many of whom, unfortunately, have neither taste nor ideas, and could do nothing but calculate the bricks wanted, and the profits to be made." Howe's assumption that women possessed an innate sense of beauty and loftier spiritual and moral inclinations than profit-minded men reflects deeply held cultural notions of femininity in the Victorian period. For Howe, women's imaginative capacities and their natural disposition "for the higher functions of life" made architecture an occupation better suited to their characters than medicine, with its study of disease and anatomical dissection, to which, she noted with dismay, her female contemporaries dedicated themselves with "so much zeal."[1]

Despite lobbying for women's inclusion in architecture, Howe was thus shaped by the ideals of her time. The finest women artists, she maintained in her speech to the Victorian Discussion Society, were also "the very best daughters, wives, and the most tender mothers." Even as they achieved success in their new vocations, these women "never forgot the broom, the frying-pans, the blankets and the sheets—those indispensable adjuncts of a comfortable household, over their paintbrushes, color, and canvas."[2] The insistence that women would not forsake hearth for career was not an uncommon assertion made by early suffragists, partly because it helped to assuage both male and female anxieties about a disruption in the "natural" order of the sexes. At the same time, many such activists genuinely believed that a woman's value, both at home and in the public sphere, was rooted in her biological differences, particularly her supposedly inborn domestic and maternal nature. Seen from this perspective, women would contribute to the greater social good by bringing their "essential" womanliness, honed by rocking the cradle and sweeping the floor, to the public sphere rather than by leaving it behind to become more like men.[3]

When, in 1880, Margaret Hicks became the first women to graduate from Cornell University's new architecture program, newspaper reports about her echoed Howe in wondering why women had not entered the profession "long ago" and in assuming that woman architects would remain closely tied to the domestic sphere—if not by brandishing a broom, then by designing the closet for it. "If anyone knows what a house should be," reported the *Washington Post*, "it is the woman who is to live in it." The *Cincinnati Enquirer* went a step further in suggesting that female designers limit their interventions to the nonpublic, housekeeping areas of the home: "If the woman architect will devote herself to kitchens and cellars, and closet-rooms and servants' sleeping-rooms, the world will be better for her appearance." Hicks herself, while not departing entirely from domestic concerns, had larger ambitions: her graduate thesis addressed tenement housing reform.[4]

Those determined, however, to keep architecture a male preserve were unwilling to make any such concessions. Opponents to integration were numerous, they often occupied powerful positions, and they were decidedly vocal in their resistance. In 1902, Thomas Raggles Davison, editor of the *British Architect*, published an article titled "May Women Practise Architecture?," in which he concluded that they may not. Like many other male

Where Are the Women Architects?

1. Katharina Pfeiffer, Germany's first female journeyman bricklayer.

critics, he assumed a chivalrous tone, presenting himself as the protector not only of architecture but of women as well. For in his view, the traits with which nature had endowed a woman and made her so irresistible to a man were precisely those that made her unsuitable for the building profession. In particular, Davison argued that women were "temperamentally unfitted" to the "production of good architectural design," their "lightness of touch," "changeability," and "charming" decorativeness lacking the masculine "strength of handling," "steadfastness of view," and "judicious reserve" needed for architecture. He maintained that "in the supreme and essential qualities of fine architecture a woman is by nature heavily handicapped." But then came the chivalrous silver lining: "May we not say—as a mere man of course—we are glad it is so, for that which is deterrent to her higher attainment in the practice of the art of architecture makes for her chiefest charm and glory as a woman."[5]

In Germany, Karl Scheffler, a popular and influential architectural critic, published a treatise on gender and creativity in 1908 in which he similarly defended the inequality of the sexes in the realm of art while largely dropping Davison's chivalrous veneer. Women who contradicted nature and recklessly pursued artistic productivity, he claimed, paid the price with their femininity. They became "irritable hermaphroditic creatures" who might suffer from a hypertrophy of the sex drive, leading to prostitution, or, more often, from lesbianism, which he warned was "terribly rife" among women artists of his day. Beyond the personal and social costs of such deviancy, the arts themselves were put at risk. This was particularly true of architecture, which Scheffler considered among the most masculine. "Woman," he thus declared, "must stay very far away from architecture."[6] Indeed, Scheffler believed that men with feminine qualities must also be discouraged from entering the field. The following year, writing about the nature of an architect's work, he emphasized the exalted masculinity required. "Our times," he asserted, "are anxious for men who are at once capable of idea and deed."[7] The architect pursues "a man's supreme yearnings" and possesses "great, masculine qualities."[8] Rugged, energetic, autocratic, he is, Scheffler contended, "a man of action."[9]

Two years later, German architect Otto Bartning echoed these sentiments in his 1911 article "Should Women Build?" Like Davison before him, Bartning was distinctly unenthusiastic about the idea, claiming that women produced feminine or weak architecture because they listened all too readily to the client. A collaborative approach to design, he insisted, undermined the masculine ideal of the architect's autonomy. In particular, Bartning rejected the participation of the housewife in the design process, arguing that her "often troublesome wishes" destroyed the "strict lawfulness" of the plan and led to the dominance of the "marginal" over the "fundamental," which he termed "feminine" architecture. In his view, strong architecture emerged from a

Where Are the Women Architects?

definitively masculine process that was necessarily adversarial: the architect realized and imposed his vision in the face of "struggles, adversity, [and] misunderstandings." Ultimately, however, Bartning was concerned less with women architects than with their insufficiently virile male colleagues. He critiqued the "weakness of our contemporary architecture," arguing that what "our architecture needs to recover is truly not female architects but rather supremely manly men."[10]

The strong resistance to women's efforts to integrate architecture, which extended beyond individuals to educational policies, school admissions, and professional associations, had a deep and lasting impact on the profession. Not only did it discourage and denigrate any so-called feminine traits in architectural practice, such as cooperation with the client, but it also raised the bar for men by producing a hypermasculine professional image defined by aggressive heterosexual virility. Howard Roark, the über-macho protagonist of Ayn Rand's hugely influential 1943 novel *The Fountainhead*, embodied the new ideal in fictional form. Roark, a "brilliant" architect, is represented as heroically violent, claiming his rights through masculine brutality. When his greatest work is defiled through compromise, he dynamites the finished building; scorned by a beautiful woman, he wins her over by a vicious sexual attack.[11] Roark was, literally, a tough act to follow, and the novel possessed a cultlike status among architectural students for decades after it was published. By exalting such "heroes," early discourses against the feminine in architecture served not only to box out women but also to box in men.[12]

Unsurprisingly, women architects resented being portrayed by their male colleagues and the media more broadly as sexual degenerates at worst and broom-closet designers at best. On rare occasions, the press itself acknowledged the discrepancy in views. "Women architects, it is said," as the Baltimore *Sun* reported in 1911, "resent the association of their names with closets. 'Just as if we couldn't build anything but closets,' one of them snapped the other day, 'and just as if any sensible man architect couldn't make all the closets that are necessary.' "[13] Women architects occasionally went to great lengths—or heights—in their attempts to shift perceptions. In 1911, for example, Fay Kellog, a successful New York City architect, insisted on being interviewed while standing on "a perilously swinging beam," nine floors up, of a skyscraper that she was constructing. When Kellog was asked whether there were any special fields particularly well suited to women in architecture, she answered, "I don't think a woman architect ought to be satisfied with small pieces, but launch out into business buildings. That is where money and name are made. I don't approve of a well-equipped woman creeping along; let her leap ahead as men do. All she needs is courage." That Kellog herself possessed such courage was emphasized by the reporter's own terrified description of the architect happily swaying high above a New York City street.[14]

Already within the first decades of entering architectural practice, women broadened their public image beyond the domestic sphere by designing buildings at worlds' fairs and other high-profile exhibitions. Most were pavilions showcasing women's work, which began to appear regularly at such fairs by the end of the nineteenth century. The widespread phenomenon of women's exhibition pavilions in the United States and Europe reflected growing efforts in Western countries to improve women's social and economic status by demonstrating in concrete, visible terms their contributions to hearth and nation. Women's buildings designed by women appeared at, among other venues, the 1893 World's Columbian Exposition in Chicago (by Sophia Hayden), the 1895 Cotton States and International Exposition in Atlanta (by Elise Mercur), the 1897 Tennessee Centennial and International Exposition (by Sara Ward-Conley), the 1913 Leipzig International Book Fair (by Emilie Winkelmann), and the 1914 German Werkbund Exhibition in Cologne (by Margarete Knüppelholz-Roeser).[15] The Haus der Frau or women's pavilion at the Werkbund Exhibition—an event considered by historians to be a watershed moment in the development of modern architecture—caused a stir because of its severe and

2. Recalling Fay Kellog in New York City, a woman builder in Berlin shows off her daring for the press. She is pictured making repairs to the roof of Berlin's City Hall in 1910.

boldly unornamented forms, prompting some design critics to argue that the pavilion's lack of "feminine grace" made it unsuitable as a women's building and to ridicule it as an architectural masquerade in men's clothing. Recalling Bartning's earlier criticism about architecture's need for supremely manly men, one vocal critic employed the masculine reputation of the women's pavilion to rebuke the male architects of the other exhibition buildings for not being, by comparison, manly enough.[16] Twenty years earlier, Hayden's design for the Woman's Building at Chicago's World's Columbian Exposition had been criticized on polar-opposite grounds. While its "femininity" was considered appropriate to a women's building, it was also blamed for producing a weak and timid impression, especially amid the other, "masterly," male-designed fair buildings.[17]

Such judgments about gender and style reveal the difficult position women architects had to navigate in avoiding accusations of designing in a manner that was excessively feminine or masculine—terms that were, in any case, elusive and highly subjective. Although, as noted earlier, the policing of architecture's gendered borders also served to discipline men, who were compelled to better perform their heterosexual masculinity, the work of male architects was rarely judged on the basis of gender alone. A notable exception was the discourse on men's failings in domestic design and the consequent need for women architects. But even there, male architects' shortcomings were blamed less on an incapacity inherent to their gender and more on men's lack of interest and expertise, which, presumably, could be remedied if they tried (although trying too hard in this respect might make their masculinity suspect). In those rare cases in which a male architect's work was criticized for being "too feminine," the flaw was typically considered to lie with the individual, not with the gender itself (hence the demands made by Bartning and others that male architects "man up"). By contrast, a woman architect who was considered a professional success was often seen to have achieved this *despite* her gender.

In the same period of exhibition building, women architects also entered and won numerous prestigious architectural competitions, further bringing attention to the broad range of women architects' work. In 1894, for example, two young women barely out of their teens, Alice Hands and Mary Gannon, who formed the United States' first female architectural partnership, won the competition for the Florence Hospital in San Francisco. When built, their design was lauded as "the finest and most practicable sanitarium on the Pacific Coast."[18] In 1907, Emilie Winkelmann, the first woman to open an architecture firm in Germany, won a competition for a large entertainment center near Alexanderplatz in Berlin. She earned high praise for her ingenious design solution for the irregular plot, which had stumped her male competitors (as the Residenz-Casino, it became one of the city's most famous dance halls of the Weimar era).[19] Two years later, in 1909, London-based Ethel Charles, the first female member of the Royal Institute of British Architects, won a competition for a church design in Berlin over two hundred other architects.[20] In 1915, another female architectural partnership, Anna Schenk and Marcia Mead, won a City Club of Chicago competition that asked architects to design an urban neighborhood center anywhere in the United States. Their project proposed a redesign of a one-mile-square area of the Bronx to provide residents with services closer to home, such as social clubs, parks, and schools.[21] In 1928, a collective gasp was heard in the architectural world when the winner of the international competition for the new Shakespeare Memorial Theater at Stratford-on-Avon, one of England's most prestigious public buildings, was revealed to be a young woman and recent graduate of the Architectural Association School in London, Elizabeth Scott. Her simple, functionalist design—an important early example of modernism in England—was selected over the proposals of seventy-one male architects competing from Canada, Britain, and the United States. Scott's victory was widely reported in the international press with headlines such as "Girl Architect Beats Men."[22]

But despite such successes, stereotypes of women architects as the profession's misfits, best consigned to domestic or interior design, proved stubbornly resistant to change. Throughout the first half of the twentieth century and into the 1960s and 1970s, appeals continued to be made in the North American and European press for women to take up architecture in order to ameliorate poorly designed housing—"like cures like," it was said.[23] Women architects had long decried the limitations of this strategy; in 1891, Louise Bethune, who had opened a highly successful architecture firm in Buffalo the previous decade, warned that house building was the "worst-paid work an architect ever does," a sentiment later echoed by Fay Kellog.[24] The housing boom in the decades after the Second World War, however, seemed to offer lucrative new possibilities to women architects who marketed themselves as domestic specialists.[25] A 1966 *Chicago Tribune* feature on Jean Wehrheim, a licensed architect with a successful residential design practice in Chicago, described her as an "attractive, vivacious young homemaker" and quoted her encouraging more women to consider a career in architecture: " 'We have a natural inclination for designing homes,' she said. 'Men seem to prefer big projects, like offices and public buildings, but I know what I am doing when it comes to designing a kitchen.' "[26]

Beginning in the 1960s, the women's liberation movement challenged women to get out of the house, and the call was felt, if somewhat belatedly, in the architectural world as well. In a 1977 *New York Times* article, "The Last Profession to Be 'Liberated' by Women," architectural critic Ada Louise Huxtable voiced her outrage that female architects were still treated as glorified housewives: "Professionally speaking, women architects have yet to get out of the kitchen. They are chained, tied and condemned to the house—to house design and house interiors in the name of design efficiency, gemütlichkeit and the family. They are supposed to know more than anyone else about kitchens and related matters, practically and symbolically, through intimate familiarity and natural concern, and they have vacillated between treating the affinity as an advantage or as a curse." Huxtable made clear that she did not demean the value of housework and family life. At the same time, she insisted that women architects' inability or unwillingness to "get away from the house" was "essentially, a dumb and minimally rewarding way to spend one's maximum designing life in the context of all architecture, and of the total built environment." She continued: "Yes, house design is important. But not that important. What is more important is that it is a limited vehicle that has led practically nowhere for women, in terms of larger architectural and environmental skills." For Huxtable, "all that pious claptrap that was preached and written from the 19th century on about women's greater domestic sensibility" had so manacled women architects' talents and professional prospects that they had distressingly little to show for a century of struggle and work.[27]

Even if one disagrees with Huxtable's assessment of the meagerness of that legacy, a look at the numbers reinforces her more general view that women architects had failed to thrive. The U.S. occupational census in 1939 revealed 379 women architects nationally. In 1949, the number had declined to 300. In 1960, women's presence had fallen even further, to an estimated 260 in architectural practice—a decline of almost a third in twenty years. By 1975, the trend had reversed, but there were still only 400 women architects nationally. As a percentage, in 1975 women represented just 1.2 percent of all licensed architects in the United States, or 3.7 percent of the entire architectural workforce. In 1926, women had made up 1 percent of all architects nationally; thus, fifty years later, there had been an increase of (at best) less than 3 percent. As one writer surveying the situation in 1977 put it, by any measure, these statistics were "ridiculous."[28]

For opponents of integration, this anemic progress simply affirmed their conviction that women had little to offer architecture. "How much is tradition and how much is biology, I don't know," Marcel Breuer stated when interviewed by Rita Reif for the *New York Times* in 1971, "but so far we just don't have great women architects." The Bauhaus-trained designer, one of the most influential voices of modernism, did hire women architects for his Madison Avenue office, who he claimed made "excellent draftsmen." But he believed there was a limit to what they could do. Architecture, he stated, "as building [conceiving the plan and supervising the construction] is too tough for women to achieve a name and success." Breuer refused to send women to construction sites, fearing that "tough" guys would create problems. Ultimately, however, it came down to husbands and babies: "I think the biggest problem of all is the biological story. Being married, being a mother is a full time job. Somehow liberation women do not want to recognize it."[29]

Breuer's female employees, interviewed by Reif for the article, admitted the difficulty of working in a masculine profession (and in Breuer's office), but beyond meeting in the company lunchroom to vent over sandwiches, there seemed to be little in the way of a united front. Given the vocal and concerted efforts already made by American women in the 1960s to fight gender discrimination, some wondered how the architectural world could remain so unaffected. In 1970, Jane Holtz Kay, then architecture critic for the *Boston Globe*, trained her lens on women architects and accused them of distancing themselves from the women's movement: "They work, some might say, in the world of the hard hat. But they wear velvet gloves and tend to speak in muted voices on the subject of Women's Lib." Kay interviewed women designers in Boston who claimed never to have experienced any prejudice and who asserted that "there'd be more militancy if there were more problems." Men and women faced the same difficulties, another stated, but women, being "too sensitive," felt "discriminated against."[30]

In 1973, Reif wrote a second article on women architects, whom she called "latecomers to the women's movement," and noted that in the interval of two years, they had begun "comparing notes and soon discovered that personal experiences of small slights and outright discrimination were shared by others."[31] Indeed, by then women architects had also begun to organize to collectively fight what they increasingly recognized as entrenched discrimination in the profession. As Gabrielle Esperdy recounts, the American Institute of Architects (AIA), the powerful U.S. national organization for architects, was challenged for being "an exclusive gentleman's club": although women had been allowed to join since 1888, when Louise Bethune became its first female member, more than eighty years later they were still discouraged from participating and had almost no visibility within the organization. At the 1973 national convention in San Francisco, a resolution on the "Status of Women in the Architectural Profession," co-authored by Judith Edelman, the first woman elected to the executive committee of the AIA's New York City chapter, called on the AIA to better integrate its female members and to take concrete action to address discrimination against female practitioners. The resolution was passed, although with considerable opposition and controversy. Accused of not acknowledging changing realities, particularly the sweeping social and legal changes bringing women into the public sphere, the AIA's male leadership insisted there was no problem. Yet when the organization, compelled by its small but vocal female membership, undertook a survey in 1974 of male and female architects to assess the status of women in the profession, a picture emerged of pervasive and deeply embedded discrimination, including lower pay for female architects, sexual harassment, and barriers to advancement. Against men's insistence on a contented and undivided profession, the survey clearly reflected women's frustration and disillusionment with the status quo.[32]

In keeping with the grassroots activism of the era, women architects formed independent groups to push for greater professional equality. The Organization of Women Architects (OWA), Chicago Women in Architecture, and the Alliance of Women in Architecture (AWA) were among the associations founded in the 1970s. Like other feminist organizations of the era, they served to raise awareness of discrimination faced by women in the workplace as well as to provide mentorship and support to their members in advancing their careers. The sense of solidarity and contact with other women in architecture was also important. Women who joined such organizations expressed how it helped them to overcome theirs feelings of isolation and of being "a freak."[33] Some of the groups, including the OWA, remain active today, their mission far from accomplished.

Not only professional organizations, but also schools, came under scrutiny in this era. Highly critical of the role academia played in maintaining and reproducing structures of power and privilege, seven women with different design backgrounds founded the Women's School of Planning and Architecture (1975–81), run by women for women. Held in summer in different locations in the United States, it offered an experimental curriculum that encouraged women to learn new skills, break free of gendered stereotypes, and explore how to use

3. Founding members of the Organization of Women Architects gathered at the San Francisco Art Institute, 1973.

architecture to help other women.[34] Feminism also began to make its influence felt within established architecture schools through special programming, such as the 1974 Women in Architecture Conference organized by female architecture students at Washington University in St. Louis and the West Coast Women's Design Conference, organized by female environmental design students and faculty and held the same year at the University of Oregon, where Denise Scott Brown spoke about sexism and architecture's "star system."[35]

The 1970s also saw the rise—at first, a mere bump—of writings about women architects. These publications mapped out their professional history (and, to the surprise of many, there was one) and addressed the issues they faced in the contemporary world of practice. Ellen Perry Berkeley's comprehensive and shocking article on the profession's rampant discrimination, which appeared in 1972 in *Architectural Forum*, politicized many women architects and catalyzed them into action.[36] The following year, Susana Torre and a small group of other women architects in New York City decided to organize an exhibition on women in their profession. They founded the Archive of Women in Architecture, housed at the Architectural League of New York headquarters, to support their planning. The extensive research they undertook was published as the groundbreaking 1977 book *Women in American Architecture: A Historic and Contemporary Perspective*, which provided a sweeping overview of a century of women's work in architecture in the United States, with a focus on the domestic. The volume, edited by Torre, also served as the catalogue for the show, which opened at the Brooklyn Museum on February 24, 1977, and was perhaps the first-ever exhibition on the history of women architects.[37] Huxtable was among the visitors, and what she saw prompted her to pen her *New York Times* article. In the same year, *Ms. Architect* appeared, representing a new style of how-to-do-it books that encouraged young women to enter male-dominated fields.[38]

The first century of debate about women in architecture thus ended on a note of promise. The second wave of feminism in the 1970s, following the first at the end of the nineteenth century, once again pushed the issues of gender discrimination in architecture to the fore, resulting in greater awareness of women's history in the profession, the challenges they continued to face, and the need to organize to effect change. At the same time, looking at the century as a whole, the progress that women had made collectively in the architectural profession toward achieving equality with their male colleagues was surprisingly limited. That is not to say that they did not contribute in significant ways to the built environment: women architects participated in the rise of modern design movements and intervened dynamically in the urban landscapes of Europe, North America, and else-where.[39] Their accomplishments and the richness of women's history in architecture more broadly should not be underestimated and are all the more astonishing given the profession's aversion to women's involvement. Nonetheless, well into the 1970s, the numbers of women in architectural practice remained tiny, and the debate about whether they could be anything more than domestic designers raged on. The profession's gendered borders remained largely intact. Although individual women had managed to break through institutional barriers over the decades, those doors quickly shut behind them, necessitating yet another pioneer to repeat the process. After many successive generations of such pioneers—representing a century of struggle, progress, and retrenchment—the question remained of how women architects could solidify and build on their gains, thus moving once and for all beyond their outsider status.

Chapter 2

The Sad State of Gender Equity in the Architectural Profession

Women currently make up 44 percent of architecture students in the United States and the United Kingdom.[1] These figures are perhaps the most hopeful sign of a more equitable future for American and British women in architecture. And yet they are also among its most troubling. How can they be both? Despite robust female enrollments in past decades, we have not seen a comparable rise in the number of women in practice, because female graduates drain out of the system. Questions about this pattern of attrition and why it continues have largely focused on women's entry into practice, particularly the early years of the transition. But the loss also suggests that not all is well in academia and that we need to better prepare female graduates for the professional conditions they will encounter. Moreover, schools themselves must be challenged on their discriminatory attitudes and practices, which architectural graduates carry forward into the workplace.

Today's enrollments in the United States would not have happened without much earlier efforts to dismantle educational barriers, including Title IX of the 1972 Education Amendments Act, which legally ended discrimination against women in federally funded education programs. Although some architecture schools, including Cornell University and the University of Illinois, began admitting women in the late nineteenth century, many did not open their doors until legally forced to do so. Architect Cassandra Carroll, interviewed by the *New York Times* in 1977, recalled that when she applied to architecture programs in the late 1950s, not a single architectural college was open to women in her native New Jersey, forcing her to move to Pennsylvania to pursue her education.[2]

Under the influence of the new legislation and the women's movement, female architectural enrollments began a steady climb. In 1972, women had made up less than 6 percent of all architecture students in the United States. By 1975, in the wake of Title IX, this figure had doubled to 14 percent. A decade later, in 1985, the percentage had again doubled and stood at a national average of 30 percent, although that number varied wildly at individual schools (from less than 7 percent to more than 50 percent). The pace of women's enrollments slowed thereafter, reaching 40 percent of all architecture students nationally by the end of the 1990s.[3] And there the numbers have largely remained, with only fractional increases in the intervening years.

In light of the enrollment gains made over the decades and antidiscrimination legislation, it would be easy to assume that architecture schools have wholly eliminated the deep and widespread discrimination against women that Ellen Perry Berkeley exposed in her 1972 "Women in Architecture" essay for *Architectural Forum*. She revealed a distressing picture of women discouraged by deans and faculty from pursuing architectural studies, critics refusing to engage with their work, male peers harassing them for taking jobs from men, and financial aid officers awarding them less funding than male students on the assumption that female students "probably" had husbands to support them.[4] Title IX changed the situation for women in theory, but practice has been another matter. In the 1990s, a series of high-profile reports in Canada and the United States revealed the hostile and even abusive environment women continued to face in some architecture schools.[5] In January 2014, the *Architects' Journal* announced that a "shocking" 54 percent of the female students responding to an international survey on the status of women in architecture claimed to have experienced sexual discrimination at university.[6]

Where Are the Women Architects?

Other forms of bias, equally widespread but more covert, are found in omissions or absences. For example, students are rarely exposed to the historic roles of women in architecture, whether as builders, clients, or critics. Admittedly, such accounts were slow to appear, emerging only in the late 1970s under the influence of the feminist movement. But the next three decades saw a true efflorescence of writings about women in architecture, even if these remained a small branch of all architecture publications. Books and articles explored women's historical roots in architecture, surveyed their professional status, and offered feminist critiques of architectural design and urban planning.[7] Writings of this period generally moved away from essentialist ideas about the relationship of biology to design—for example, that men design phallic towers, while women are drawn to curvaceous and womblike shapes—although such views have not entirely disappeared, as recent criticisms of Zaha Hadid's Al Wakrah Stadium in Qatar as "a great vulvic bulge" reveal.[8] The early 1990s also saw the emergence of an architectural theory of gender that examined gendered values in architecture's modes of analysis and its language, such as in the treatment of structure as masculine and decoration as feminine.[9]

Today these many decades of research and publications amount to a substantial and significant body of literature on women and gender in architecture. Yet its impact remains limited because the knowledge and insights it offers rarely find their way into the curricula of architecture schools, where they are arguably most needed. The 1980s and 1990s witnessed a profound transformation of the humanities and social sciences curricula at North American and European universities. Today it would be shocking to find, for example, a survey course on the history of world art or on cultural theory that did not include a single female name. And yet this is routinely the case with history and theory courses offered in architecture schools.[10] In light of such glaring omissions, one can no longer argue that the necessary material is not available; it is there in abundance. But for it to find its way onto syllabi—to be lifted off the library shelf

and actually put into use—there must be a desire to shift peda-
gogical gears.

Similarly, design studios that make gender or women their
focal point are almost nonexistent in architecture schools. The
studio curriculum, which is at the heart of any architectural
program, is largely shaped by the interests and experiences of
faculty members. Although it is simplistic to assume that female
faculty will be interested in courses relating to women and that
male faculty will not, nonetheless, the gender imbalance among
design faculty at architecture schools has almost certainly
contributed to the absence of such themes in studio courses.
A female student responding to the 2014 *Architects' Journal*
survey complained, "There aren't enough women teaching—it is
very male dominated."[11] In the United States, about a quarter of
all tenured professors in architecture schools are women.[12] This
percentage encompasses all specializations, including history
and theory, which have a higher representation of women. In
many schools, the presence of women among the ranks of tenured design faculty remains negligible. Because design studios,
especially the more prestigious upper-level undergraduate and
graduate courses, tend to be assigned according to seniority,
the gender imbalance among tenured design faculty results
in the overwhelming majority of such courses being taught by
men.[13] Moreover, nontenured female faculty who teach studio
courses are much less likely to risk a "controversial" theme.

Several years ago, at one of the nation's top architecture
schools, a female tenured design professor offered an undergraduate studio that addressed a pressing social need: housing for
survivors of domestic violence. The theme was truly exceptional
for an architecture school, a provocative gesture in a milieu
where faculty and students typically shun courses perceived as
feminist. And yet, although highly unusual, the material could
hardly be said to be irrelevant: architects have an important
role to play in creating environments that promote a sense of
security and healing for the occupants, and the studio offered
students a chance to combine design and social justice concerns.

At the end of the semester, I participated in the final review as the only woman on a panel of five guest critics. Over the course of the three-hour review, the male critics discussed the formal aspects of the designs but did not once refer to the function of the proposed buildings or to their users. They could have been discussing anything—parking structures, fire stations, coffee shops, cinemas—take your pick. Whether from discomfort, ignorance, or a lack of interest, they thus removed the projects from their intention and context, abstracting them to an assemblage of architectural elements. The challenge of designing spaces for a highly vulnerable population suffering from severe trauma was left unexplored. It was almost as if there were no language in this architectural milieu with which to discuss it.

The conversations that do not happen in architecture schools also extend to public lecture series. These talks are an integral part of the pedagogy of architecture schools, a way to promote intellectual exchange and to expose students and faculty to "luminaries" of the profession. Additionally, they are a time for the school's community, both academic and beyond, to come together and engage in broader discussions. Lori Brown and Nina Freedman, co-founders of the New York City–based advocacy group ArchiteXX, surveyed the public lecture series at seventy-three architecture schools in the United States during the 2012–13 academic year. They discovered that in the fall, 62 percent of the schools had invited just one woman or no women at all to speak. The following spring, over a third had no women on their lecture podiums.[14] Privileging male voices in this way sends a strong message about who a school considers an authority and deems worthy of an audience. It also discourages female students. As one student-respondent to the 2014 *Architects' Journal* survey stated, "Women architects are never discussed or celebrated in school. It is almost perceived as a negative to be a woman in architecture."[15]

But even these statistics are misleading as indicators of exposure to gender issues per se in architecture schools. Most women architects invited to speak about their work choose not to discuss their experiences in the field as women. And one could argue, why should they? A male architect, after all, would not be expected to reflect on being a man in the profession (although it probably would be a good thing if he were). But if these women do not speak out, who will? Lectures that specifically address women in architecture, whether in terms of contemporary issues or their histories, are in short supply on the architecture lecture circuit. This silence is particularly astonishing at a time when the status of women has become a public relations nightmare for the profession, with a deluge of negative stories appearing in the press and online blogs. You wouldn't know it, though, from the discussions happening—or rather, not happening—inside architecture schools.

Unsurprisingly, women leave architecture school poorly prepared for the gender discrimination they will face in the professional world. Recent studies support what women architects have been saying for years: in terms of job opportunities, pay equity, mentoring, and promotion, the deck is stacked against them. This contributes to an appalling and enduring phenomenon: the massive drop-out of women architects from practice. Although the proportion of women has grown from a third to 42 percent of architecture school graduates in the United States in the past fifteen years, their numbers in practice have climbed at a glacial pace. In 2000, women represented 13 percent of registered architects; today that number stands at 19 percent.[16] If this rate of progress holds, we will have to wait until 2093 before we reach a 50–50 gender split. Although the numbers vary somewhat, this pattern of attrition also holds true for other countries, including England and Australia. More than a glass ceiling, there would appear to be a massive, choking bottleneck squeezing women out of practice. Since the 1990s, the question of "Where are the women architects?" has surfaced repeatedly in the media in response to this disappearance. Studies of the phenomenon that attempt to provide an answer, and that have been initiated by women themselves, suggest that the root of the problem is not what most people think.

In 1908, German architectural critic Karl Scheffler insisted that creative productivity and human reproductivity did not mix. The assumption lives on, and to the question "Where are the women architects?," the facile response has been "At home, having babies." This explanation has never been able to account for the women who choose not to have children but leave architecture anyway. Nor do mothers in architecture who leave necessarily do so because of their children. Nonetheless, the perception remains that having a baby will damage a woman's architectural career. The 2014 *Architects' Journal* survey revealed widespread anxiety among women about the professional consequences of maternity—88 percent believed it would have a negative impact. (By contrast, 62 percent of men believed that having children would have no affect at all on a father's career.) In an example of life imitating art, one of the respondents admitted that—like Michelle Pfeiffer's architect character in the 1996 film *One Fine Day*—"she had hidden the fact she had kids from her employer 'for fear it would hinder her career.' "[17] Unfortunately, women's anxieties are not unfounded. Architecture perceives itself as an all-or-nothing profession, and part-time or flexible work schemes are discouraged, adding to parents' burdens in juggling family and work.[18] Employers all too often expect pregnant architects to leave or lose interest in their work and demote or sideline them accordingly; women report returning from maternity leave to find their positions stripped of their former appeal and interest—not by their babies but by their bosses, who assume they are unable to continue with their usual responsibilities. Others discover that their jobs have vanished altogether.[19] And yet, even taking into account these obstacles, only a fraction (3.8 percent) of the *Architects' Journal* survey's female respondents stated that parenthood resulted in their leaving architecture altogether.[20]

Instead, it is the pervasive and deeply rooted inequality of professional opportunities and treatment as well as a male-dominated workplace culture that lie at the heart of most women's exodus from architecture. The factors are complex and tend to be multiple and varied—not a single event but, as architect Deborah Berke explains, the "recurring small blows" or "death by a thousand cuts" that pushes women out the door.[21] Moreover, recent studies suggest that, rather than one large bottleneck, there are various "pinch points" along the trajectory of a woman architect's career, such as in pursuing licensure or hitting the glass ceiling, where attrition is more likely to occur.[22]

In an effort to understand and combat women's high dropout rates, in 2013 members of the San Francisco chapter of the AIA created "The Missing 32% Project," named after the percentage of female architecture graduates who are lost to practice. As part of its research mission, the project surveyed nearly twenty-three hundred male and female architects nationally and found that job satisfaction was notably lower among women (28 percent) than men (41 percent). The reasons are not hard to discern. There is, to begin with, a pronounced difference in what men and women earn. In a profession known for its long hours and low compensation, this issue hits hard. The pay gap exists at all levels, from entry-level positions to principals, but increases sharply at midcareer. For example, the Missing 32% Project reported that male architects with fifteen to twenty years of experience earned on average $100,000, whereas women with the same level of experience earned $80,000. In 2014 the U.S. Bureau of Labor Statistics also found that, among full-time architects, men earn on average 20 percent more than women. The 2014 survey by the *Architects' Journal* suggests that the imbalance is even greater and calls the pay gap "the most effective barometer of gender inequality in the profession." But because salary transparency is rare in most firms, the extent of these disparities is usually hidden. As the journal noted, many women who responded to their survey grossly underestimated how much more their male colleagues were earning.[23]

Folded within this salary gap is another story about women architects and stalled promotions that also contributes significantly to job dissatisfaction and dropping out. According to national AIA records, the numbers of women principals

Where Are the Women Architects?

WHERE ARE THE WOMEN IN ARCHITECTURE?

4. Graphic used to advertise the Missing 32% Symposium organized by the American Institute of Architects, San Francisco Chapter (AIASF), and held on October 13, 2012. The event was the second in a longer series of meetings, begun in 2011, that led to the creation in 2013 of the Missing 32% Project (since renamed Equity by Design) to investigate the status of women in the architectural profession.

and partners at firms quadrupled from 4 percent in 1999 to 16 percent in 2005. What seemed to be a breakthrough in women's professional ascent soon proved, however, to be another instance of stagnation: a decade later, the figure stands at 17 percent.[24] The National Council of Architectural Registration Boards, which administers registration examinations and develops internship programs in the United States, reports that women represent only 13 percent of supervisors in architecture firms who are overseeing interns. Stated differently, 87 percent of young architects working toward licensure are doing so with a male supervisor, at least according to the official record.[25]

Various factors contribute to women's slow professional climb up the architectural ladder. Maternity is often seen as the chief culprit, and many women with children do express frustration at the profession's "mommy track," with its diminished opportunities. But, as architect Diana Griffiths writes, "if family commitments were the only barrier to success then women architects without children should be thriving" and "flying through the ranks."[26] That they are not indicates that there are other, broader impediments. Among them, women are less likely to receive the more glamorous types of projects that help to advance careers. This is often blamed on women themselves: they lack the ambition to go after the big jobs, it is said, or are unwilling to put in the long hours required to pay their dues. The underlying presumption here, deeply engrained in the professional culture, is that architecture is a meritocracy that rewards talent and hard work in a straightforward way.[27] Women who share that belief and commit themselves to architectural practice without seeing professional returns are apt to lose confidence in their own abilities. As Denise Scott Brown has written, "On seeing their male colleagues draw out in front of them, women who lack a feminist awareness are likely to feel that their failure to achieve is their own fault."[28]

Mentoring can make a critical difference: careers are advanced not just by ambition and sacrifice but also by having a sponsor to show you the ropes, make connections, and put your name forward for those career-enhancing opportunities. The first attrition pinch points for a woman come in the early years after she graduates from an architecture program, when she struggles to make the transition to practice. As an intern working toward licensure, she will rely for guidance and support on a pool of architectural supervisors that, as noted earlier, is 87 percent male. Later in her career, as she strives to break through the glass ceiling— another attrition pinch point—she will be dependent on finding mentors among a leadership that is 83 percent male (based on the gender breakdown of partners and principals). Women in male-dominated fields benefit from having a mentor, whether it is a man or a woman. But, as Sheryl Sandberg writes in *Lean In*, "Men are significantly more likely than women to be sponsored." Moreover, mentors tend to choose protégés who remind them of themselves.[29]

A few years ago, I met with a group of women at a prestigious global architecture firm that has an almost exclusively male leadership. The women, despite degrees from the nation's top architecture schools and years of hard work—they ate not only lunches but also dinners at their desks (and none had children)—had not advanced significantly up the firm's corporate ladder. They described an office culture deeply shaped by an "old boys' club" mentality. It was customary, for example, for the male partners to informally select an incoming young architect to mentor and bring up through the ranks, a process that included plum assignments, invitations to important meetings, and introductions to prestigious clients. Among the women, the protégé was known as "the anointed one," and in their time at the firm they had never seen the honor bestowed on a woman. Meanwhile, the very few women in senior management offered little support. Speaking as a female executive who finds direct requests for mentorship "a total mood killer," Sandberg cautions young women not to be too aggressive in this pursuit and advises them instead to focus on excelling, which will draw mentors to them.[30] Yet women can excel day after day, year after year, and still remain invisible in a system that sees only men as leadership material.

Beyond low pay and stalled careers, job satisfaction for women architects is eroded by routine sexism in the workplace. The "Women in Architecture" surveys published annually by the *Architects' Journal*, beginning in 2012, suggest that the problem is widespread and getting worse. The survey asks: "Have you ever suffered sexual discrimination in your career in architecture? (This might include inappropriate comments, or being treated differently because of your gender.)" In 2012, 63 percent of the 700 female respondents answered in the affirmative. Some online commenters have objected to the breadth and subjectivity of the question, arguing that holding a door open for a woman or giving her maternity leave could qualify under this definition. But the examples submitted by respondents indicate that they know what discrimination means. These include being given more secretarial work to do than male peers, being asked whether they are menstruating, and being told that pregnancy will result in a salary cut. In the 2014 survey, 66 percent of the 710 female respondents answered in the affirmative. These accounts cannot be dismissed as tales of the dark past: most respondents are young—80 percent are under the age of forty. Moreover, the discrimination continues, for some on a regular basis: 33 percent encounter it on a monthly or quarterly basis, while 11 percent say it is a daily or weekly occurrence.[31]

The more overt forms of sexism tend to occur in work with contractors, and two-thirds of the female respondents to the 2014 *Architects' Journal* survey felt that women's authority has yet to be accepted in the building industry, with half of the male respondents agreeing. When women first entered architecture in the nineteenth century, their opponents claimed that they would be defeated by their lack of authority on the construction site, a claim that is still used to justify women's lower promotion rates compared to men. But as Patricia Hickey, co-founder of Bubble Architects, stated in response to the survey, "We need to be clear that women are being held back from promotion in architectural offices not because the practice directors think they will not be respected on site, but because the primarily male directors do not respect female leaders within the office; otherwise a gender pay discrepancy for the same roles would not persist."[32] A number of studies suggest that it is easier for women architects to develop coping strategies for the overt sexism they may encounter at the building site. By contrast, the more subtle and pervasive forms of discrimination encountered in the architectural office do more damage because they are harder to counteract or defend against.[33]

As a historian, what alarms me about this picture—beyond the legacies that have been lost to us and the sheer injustice of it—is how familiar it all is. For well over a hundred years, in one form or another, women architects have been fighting the same battle. In 1905, for example, Mabel Brown interviewed women architects for the *San Francisco Chronicle* to discover why they remained "something of a curiosity." She was told "that popular prejudice is against women architects—that it is next to impossible for one to get an opening in a regular office; and since experience means everything, it is impossible to make headway when denied a beginning."[34] Resistance to their employment, as we know from other sources in this period, was based on fear that a female presence would disrupt a male environment, skepticism about their training and skills, the certainty that they could not exercise authority on the building site, and the assumption that their commitment to practice would evaporate as soon as they married.[35] If a woman did manage to get her foot in the door, Brown learned, she could expect menial duties and a "pittance" for pay. Architectural offices typically assigned women drafting or detail work, because they were believed to lack the "all-round" skills of their male colleagues.[36] To avoid such constraints, women architects advised other women considering the profession to open their own firms. But they also warned them to think twice about pursuing architecture at all if they lacked "the influence necessary to get on," meaning the personal and professional networks for success.[37] By and large, the hurdles to equity a hundred years ago sound strikingly similar to those encountered today.

At the same time, 2015 is not 1905. Laws now protect against discrimination, even if they are not always enforced, and women architects have the numbers and allies to push for real change. The latter include male architects also dissatisfied with the status quo. The 2014 *Architects' Journal* survey revealed that 73 percent of the male respondents (and 79 percent of the women) believe the profession is too male.[38] Moreover, although there have long been global forms of communication, the accessibility and reach of the Internet have both revealed how widespread the problem is and created the possibility for meaningful collaborations across borders and cultures. Finally, studies on gender discrimination in architecture, some of which have been cited here, have proliferated in recent years. In some cases, they provide us with concrete recommendations for tackling architecture's gender inequities, whereas in others, they highlight new areas of research that still need to be explored.

While money is not a panacea for architecture's gender inequities, it is a good place to start. Professional organizations must step up and exert pressure to end illegal pay practices. In the United Kingdom, architects are calling on the Royal Institute of British Architects (RIBA) to "name and shame" firms that pay women less than men for similar work, saying that it is no longer enough to issue general statements of condemnation. The demand arose after a report was released by the U.K. Office for National Statistics indicating that women architects earn 25 percent less on average than their male counterparts. Those denouncing the pay divide argue that change will not happen until the culprits are exposed and that inaction suggests indifference or even acquiescence. As Stephen Riley of Kiran Curtis Associates stated, "This issue has been raised constantly over the past 30 years and [the RIBA] is now looking rather foolish and damaging the image of the profession."[39]

Persuasion of a different sort has been explored by the Beverly Willis Architecture Foundation (BWAF) in encouraging large firms to take responsibility for promoting diversity among their leadership ranks. Beverly Willis, who opened an architecture office in San Francisco in 1958, founded BWAF in New York City in 2002 to advance women's status in the building industry. Since 2010, she and others at the BWAF have been holding round table forums with industry leaders as a means to educate them about the importance of diversity in senior management. The participants include principals or partners and human resource executives of the nation's largest architecture, engineering, and construction firms. In addition, the BWAF invites female executives from the organizations representing their most important clients. The mix is an effective one. When companies know that their clients are mindful of their lack of diversity, they become much more motivated to institute changes to protect their image and bottom line.[40] Professional architecture organizations, such as the AIA, have an important role to play here in setting and promoting strong industry norms. Without such pressures, the status quo is likely to continue, with the anointed of one generation passing the baton to the anointed of the next.

Female role models can exert their own influence and need to be far more visible in classrooms, firms, and professional organizations. Having a personal relationship with a role model is not necessary; an effective role model may be a prominent figure in the profession or even a historical one. Role models boost self-esteem by countering negative stereotypes that cast doubt on a person's abilities to perform well in the profession. They increase motivation for career advancement and success. They foster a sense of identification with a field, combating alienation. The scarcity of female role models in architecture is thus profoundly damaging. According to the Missing 32% Project, almost a third of women who left practice gave the lack of role models as the deciding factor.[41]

To date, studies conducted on the status of women architects have largely focused on countries where attrition rates have been high, including Australia, Canada, the United Kingdom, and the United States. In addition to this national research, we need cross-cultural investigations that would allow us to compare places where women architects languish with those where they thrive. Among the latter is Greece, which by 1967 had seen women's architectural enrollments at the National Technical University in Athens reach 70 percent. That same year, women represented 50 percent of practitioners in Greece; today they are in the majority (58 percent). What makes Greece a welcoming environment for women in comparison to, say, Estonia, where 85 percent of architects are men?[42] Along similar lines, what makes architecture different from other demanding and traditionally male occupations, such as medicine and law, in which women experience greater success? Women currently represent a third of all doctors and lawyers in the United States, and those numbers are moving closer toward parity: half of the youngest doctors and lawyers are women.[43] Our understanding of what holds women back in architecture would benefit from comparative studies with other professions that have better integrated and retained their female practitioners. An extensive literature on gender diversity and women's leadership exists for other fields, but the lack of comprehensive long-term data for architecture has limited the ability to engage with it in order to determine what conditions are specific to the profession, and where it can implement successful strategies developed by others.[44] Studies of this scale require considerable resources, however, and architecture's professional organizations have been slow to take the initiative.

That may change as their members become more vocal in demanding greater gender equity in architecture. Among the highlights of the 2015 AIA National Convention in Atlanta was a "hackathon" workshop organized by Equity by Design (formerly known as the Missing 32% Project) that brought together women and men from diverse backgrounds in a shared search for solutions. Many of those present had become interested in the issues through Equity by Design's social media outreach and were meeting for the first time at the convention, reinforcing the role that new forms of networking are having in knitting activist individuals and groups into a larger and more powerful movement. Equity by Design also displayed its research findings on gender equity issues, making visible, through its bold infographics, the impact of discrimination on the careers of women architects. Additionally, Rosa Sheng, the group's founding chair, co-authored a resolution for "Equity in Architecture," overwhelmingly passed by the convention delegates, that calls on "both women and men to realize the goal of equitable practice in order to retain talent, advance the architecture profession, and communicate the value of design to society" and states that "equity is everyone's issue." As the resolution points out, although the institute has recently called on the public to "look up" and value architecture and the service architects provide to society, the profession itself needs to look inward and to reflect on why it so devalues its own "human capital." The resolution calls on the institute "to develop an ongoing program to assess data, set a plan of action, track progress, and report on results. Now more than ever is the time for action both from grassroots and Institute leadership." As the resolution itself underscores, there have been many similar resolutions passed over the years—the first, as noted in chapter 1, at the 1973 AIA convention in San Francisco, over forty years ago.[45] Whether the leadership of the AIA and other professional organizations will finally take up their members' calls for action and address architecture's ongoing diversity problems through courageous and effective policy actions remains to be seen.

Chapter 3

What I Learned from Architect Barbie

In February 2011, Architect Barbie made her industry debut at the Toy Industry Association's Toy Fair in New York City; three months later, she made her professional entrance at the AIA convention in New Orleans. But Architect Barbie's real beginnings were political. In 2006, while I was a research fellow at the University of Michigan, the passage of Proposal 2, a ballot initiative, ended affirmative action in that state.[1] Debates before and after the law's passage tore into friendships and collegial relationships, and the atmosphere on campus was tense as the school's colleges, including architecture, struggled to determine what the new law would mean for diversity among students and faculty and, ultimately, why that diversity mattered.

The question was a pressing one for architecture, even if the profession had done its best to ignore it. Certainly there had been past instances of vocal and public confrontation with architecture's exclusions, such as at the 1973 AIA convention, when female members protested their marginalization.[2] By the mid-2000s, there was also a substantial literature on architecture's gender issues. But the cumulative impact of these many decades of effort remained surprisingly limited. One could not speak, in 2006, of a broad consciousness within the profession or among the public of how or why architecture continued to drive out women.

As a feminist scholar, I am interested in analyzing the ideological fences that architecture has built around the profession— the barriers that determine outsiders and insiders. One starting point is the idealized image of the architect that has been nurtured within the profession and reinforced in popular culture. Here we find a pervasive insistence on the incompatibility of the

5. Architect Barbie on display at the American Institute of Architects Convention in New Orleans, May 2011.

architectural and the feminine—seen not only in early twentieth-century writings on modern architecture by Otto Bartning, Karl Scheffler, and others, but also in Hollywood films, such as *One Fine Day* (1996), in which Michelle Pfeiffer, playing an architect compelled to bring her young child to work, trips over her own handbag and crushes the design model she is carrying, including its phallic high-rise. This scene also points to another deeply embedded conflict in the image of the architect: the irreconcilability of production and reproduction. They require different and opposing abilities, we are told, and being a good architect necessarily means being a bad parent, as Adam Sandler's character discovered in *Click* (2006).[3]

Hoping to encourage discussion about these beliefs and attitudes, but wary of preaching to the converted, I looked for an unusual angle from which to address issues of diversity in my fellowship exhibition at Michigan, held in the spring of 2007. I had long admired feminist artists, such as the Guerrilla Girls, who use humor to political ends.[4] Given the tensions and resentments stirring on campus in the wake of Prop 2, it seemed more important than ever to harness the disarming power of humor. It was at that point that I remembered Architect Barbie. In 2002, Mattel had staged a public vote to allow people to determine the next career in its new professional series, "Barbie I Can Be . . . ." The choices—architect, librarian, and police woman—unleashed an epic online battle, which Architect Barbie won. But, to the disappointment of her supporters, Mattel would not commit to producing the doll. Julia Jensen, then Mattel spokesperson, explained that a little girl did not think in complex professional terms when she imagined her mother at work. From a child's perspective, "she drinks coffee," Jensen said, "she is on the phone all day." Being an architect "is not in their lexicon."[5]

Eager to see Architect Barbie materialize, I asked Michigan architecture students and faculty to develop their own prototypes. I was particularly interested in how a younger generation, just learning to become architects and absorbing the professional culture, would imagine her. The results, exhibited in the architecture school, were an eye-opener. I had expected Barbie to show up in a black power suit and Corbusier eyeglasses. In other words, architecture would come first, Barbie second. Instead, some students reversed the order. Their dolls explored architecture on Barbie's own terms, from an über-feminine angle that celebrated fashion, hairstyles, and makeup. In these dolls I was confronted by the "femmenism" or "girl (grrrl) power" of a younger generation that seeks empowerment by playing up femininity in contexts that prohibit it. Inside architecture's hallowed halls, Barbie's "girlie" attributes were a mark not of oppression but of resistance. These dolls looked you right in the eye and asked, "Why can't architects wear pink?"

My assumptions would be challenged again a few years later, when Architect Barbie finally entered the realm of trademarked toys. In February 2010, Mattel invited the public to vote on

6. A glimpse of the Architect Barbie exhibition (left) held at the University of Michigan in the spring of 2007, with architecture students outside the gallery on their way to class.

Barbie's 125th career, its first such election since the miscarriage of 2002. Having once shunned "complex" careers in the "Barbie I Can Be . . ." line, Mattel was now focusing on professions in which women were underrepresented. (Even a corporation can evolve.) This time, Architect Barbie's rivals included Surgeon Barbie and Computer Engineer Barbie; the latter emerged victorious.[6] At this point—still reluctant to concede defeat—I joined forces with architect Kelly Hayes McAlonie, a colleague at the University at Buffalo, in a last-ditch effort to save Architect Barbie, and we approached Mattel directly to advocate for the doll. To our delighted surprise, Kelly and I were asked to advise on her design.

Over the next six months, as Mattel explored the world of architecture, Kelly and I were inducted into the mysteries of toy manufacturing. One of our first lessons was that creating Barbie in the image of a professional was not about miniaturizing the adult world but rather about translating it into a child's terms. Yes, we know architects like to wear black (we like it ourselves). But to a five-year-old girl, a doll dressed in black says "villain" or "morti-cian," not "architect." In working with Amy Lee, Mattel's designer, on Architect Barbie's outfit, we focused on simple volumes, clean lines, and basic colors. Because Barbie's molded feet made flats impossible, we gave her black ankle boots with a chunky heel. With architecture undergoing rapid changes, not least in its tech-nologies, accessorizing Barbie involved difficult choices. We sent a list of twenty-five possible accessories to our Mattel collaborators, who selected three with iconic power and instant recognizability: a pink drawing tube, white hard hat, and black glasses.

Negotiating the transition from office to construction site also posed a sartorial challenge. What outfit would work for both? After considering slacks, we ultimately agreed with Mattel that Architect Barbie would wear a dress. A century ago, men campaigned to ban women from construction sites because their dresses (standing in for female bodies) were seen as nuisances. Given that women then were also forbidden to wear pants, this dress code effectively excluded them from the building trades.[7] Our decision to combine a hard hat with a dress—symbols of building and femininity—channeled the spirit of girl power, flaunting that which has been prohibited.

Little did we realize what we were about to unleash. In February, the doll's unveiling at the Toy Fair produced the first of what would grow to be nearly three hundred media stories, including twenty television segments, by mid-autumn, resulting in 175 million media impressions.[8] In December, the *Guard-ian*, *Building Design*, and *USA Network* included her in their top architectural stories or lists of 2011, and she made the *Wall Street Journal*'s holiday "hot stuff" survey.[9] The *Architects' Jour-nal* in the United Kingdom put her on the cover of its first-ever issue devoted to women in architecture. She was featured in *Elle Decor* and even earned a mention in *Vogue*.[10] Kelly and I watched all of this unfold, amazed.

For some, Architect Barbie was cause for celebration. Readers of *Jezebel*, a self-styled part feminist, part celebrity and fashion news blog, embraced her when the news broke in February. "Not since Mike Brady was supposed to be an architect of suburban houses that all looked like gas stations," wrote asp in the comments section, "has my chosen profession seemed so flirty and glam." Another self-identified architect, hottotrot, admitted, "I would pay big money for a hot pink drawing tube." A covetous Anita Drink posted, "God help me, I really love Barbie's outfit, and I want it for myself!" Barbie's girlie disregard for architectural conventions was not lost on *Jezebel*'s audience. "Not so much inspired by Howard Roark, I see," wrote bettylyons.[11]

Others greeted Architect Barbie with scorn. An announcement about the doll on the website of Australian-based *Indesign* magazine elicited mostly negative responses in the comments section. "Everyone knows that real architects only wear black," objected Dinah. "The hard hat is useless," wrote Skye, "as they'll never let her on site in those heels!" Mat said, "She looks like a first year student of architecture that will fail and become a nail designer after crying all over her blueprints for 3 months first." A poster called real architect responded, "Looks more like an interior designer/decorator than an architect." Brightbeam added, "Architect Barbie, displaying the d**b blond look."[12]

Some of the criticism directed against the doll clearly targeted the profession's own gender problems. Sarah, an architect commenting on Nancy Levinson's *Design Observer* blog post, wrote: "Architect Barbie couldn't wear such a skimpy outfit to the office, which is inevitably full of old men or to the construction site which is full of construction workers. She would wear faded black pants and a shirt that is wrinkled from sleeping under her desk. Her teeth would be bad because she won't have dental insurance and her stomach would be pouchy from a bad diet hurriedly scarfed down at her desk. Her accessories should include a paycheck that is 30% less than the men's, antidepressants, and IBS medication."[13]

Barbie's grown-up brand of femininity, which distinguished her from traditional baby dolls when she was launched in 1959, has been fiercely debated by scholars for decades. Her champions point to Barbie's rebellious side and her preference for independence and a career over marriage. Although some of her employment choices have been stereotypical, others have been daring (NASCAR Barbie) as well as lucrative, allowing her to own a house, a Ferrari, and a Porsche. She also enjoys adventure and travel and has been known to hop on her Hot Stylin' Motorcycle and head for the open road. Her critics, by contrast, argue that the doll's lifestyle equates happiness with materialism and teaches girls to consume, while her "preposterous physique" encourages eating disorders.[14] Peggy Orenstein and others have also criticized the gendering of color choices and the dominance of pink merchandise for girls.[15]

The oft-made critiques on design blogs about Architect Barbie's being too blond (the African American model attracted little attention), wearing clothing with too much color—especially pink—as well as too much makeup, and being prone to assaults or accidents due to her dress and ankle boots provoked angry responses regarding assumptions about what an architect looks like and what earns respect on the job. Some welcomed Barbie's "audacious" challenge to stereotypes and suggested that architecture clung to the old tropes because it had lost a sense of its own identity.[16] Others commented on the lack of role models and wondered whether Architect Barbie or LEGO blocks could better inspire girls to become builders.[17]

As the discourse about Architect Barbie unfolded, it became clear that a good deal of the tension was not between men and women but rather between women of different ages. In her power as a cultural icon and the feelings of love or hate she evokes, Barbie had exposed, in a way not previously seen, a generational divide between women in architecture that went far beyond the merits of a doll. This was clearly visible in the long and heated discussion thread "Fetish in Pink" initiated by Inda in March 2011 on the AIA LinkedIn forum. Inda wrote:

Women of a certain age, i.e. my generation, know what the feminist revolution was really all about and what Barbie symbolizes. Barbie is a sexist symbol. Our colleagues must be very, very careful with this issue. Promoting architecture in a sexist way with a sexist venue is not good for any of us, male or female.

Many of us who grew up and marched in the streets in the turbulent times of the 60s and 70s never gave our children Barbie dolls . . . and that was on principle. You must realize that the Barbie doll is a vestigial symbol of the time when women were not accepted in the field of architecture. Across our society we are currently suffering a swing of the pendulum back to the time before feminism. Do you all really romanticize the "Mad Men" era?

Adriana, who identified herself as thirty-five, responded: "Lighten up! They are dolls, not realistic representations of women. I had lots of Barbies growing up and played with them until I was 12. I didn't think I was supposed to look like a cabbage patch kid any more than a Barbie." Leslie shared her exasperation: "WTF to those negative, bitter people against Barbie. I dressed them up and created houses and neighborhoods with the cases they came in. I didn't view them as 'sexist' objects and still don't, but rather as toys that helped me explore my creative side. It's unfortunate that some 'naïve' people just don't get it." Laura responded: "I am glad that there are young women architects who find nothing offensive in this Barbie. However, this discussion is not only about a doll. I wish I could see Barbie as beautiful. She is NOT. She is a gross misrepresentation of what women look like. There are NO real women who have her dimensions. Of course, for boys, Ken and GI Joe are both disturbingly missing an important member!" (A male poster asked if they were missing their beer guts.) Inda added: "Many of the younger architects don't really get it about Barbie's image. So be it. Continues to prove that progress is elusive."[18]

A similar generational crevasse appeared in the comments section of Levinson's *Design Observer* blog post. Tracey, who opened her own architecture firm in the mid-1980s, called

Architect Barbie's image "regressive." Patricia, of the same generation and also founder of a firm, expressed dismay at the doll's "degrading outmoded message, 'Women need to be sexy to get ahead.'" These comments elicited a sharp response from Ellie, who clearly felt talked down to by the older posters. She wrote, "I think Architect Barbie is absolutely fantastic!!! Get off your high horses all you old women who think this is regressive; why should young female architects have to subscribe to masculine traits and pseudo-intellectual dress codes in order to be taken seriously? I have no problem wearing short skirts and stockings; indeed, when I do turn up to the site in such attire, I find the contractors pay attention to my every word . . . rock on Barbie!"[19]

Internet forums are not always the place for subtle discussions. Still, I found these exchanges troubling because there seemed to be so little middle ground. Moreover, they hinted at deeper fissures of mistrust between generations of women architects. Older posters claimed that a younger generation of female architects did not understand what was truly at stake, thus putting the "real" feminist revolution at risk. Younger posters defining their professional identities and strategies, in turn, treated older women as irrelevant at best and oppressive at worst.

I suspect that even if Barbie were not in the picture, Inda would not see eye to eye with Ellie. One could argue that this is not a problem. Generations typically chafe against and provoke one another, don't they? I certainly learned a great deal from my "shocking" students at the University of Michigan and their grrrl politics. Yet healthy progress depends on finding a way forward that does not empower one generation at the expense of another. As the 2013 Denise Scott Brown Pritzker Prize petition, discussed in chapter 4, has demonstrated, there can be great unity across generations, with the second and third waves of feminists supporting one another's agendas. At the same time, and as I learned from Architect Barbie, that solidarity cannot be assumed but must also be built.

That process of cross-generational coalition making was on view at the "Ladies (and Gents) Who Lunch with Architect

Barbie" event organized in October 2011 by the AIA San Francisco Chapter to discuss women's status in architecture, the impact of Architect Barbie on professional stereotypes, and what it takes to succeed in the profession.[20] At the sold-out symposium, a panel of women architects in various professional roles and at different stages of their careers shared their views of the doll. Here, too, opinion was divided along generational lines, but the lively conversation ultimately helped to forge new alliances.[21] The popularity of the event led the following year to the Missing 32% Symposium, which focused on retaining and promoting women in architecture and which, in turn, launched Equity by Design, the project that has now taken a leading role in studying and discussing the future of women in the profession.[22]

Lisa Boquiren, a lead organizer of the "Ladies (and Gents)" event, called Architect Barbie "the lightning rod" for long-standing tensions about gender that had never been adequately addressed within the profession. "How better to start a conversation about the problem of women's low participation in the very male-dominated profession of architecture than through a globally-influential American icon?," she asked.[23] Yet as much as Kelly and I rejoiced over the breaking of the silence—which had felt so much more intolerable than any raucous debate— ultimately we had another audience in mind for whom we hoped to harness Barbie's electrifying power.

After all of the fuss over clothes and hairstyles and accessories, what mattered most to girls about Architect Barbie was her *Dasein*—her being in and of their everyday world. And this, Architect Barbie's last and most enduring lesson, became fully clear to me only at the official launch of the doll, at the AIA convention in New Orleans. Working with Mattel and the AIA, Kelly and I developed workshops for four hundred girls recruited from local schools and girls' clubs. The workshops, led by women architects, had three components: an introduction to what architects do, a discussion of the work of past and present women architects, and an exercise to redesign Barbie's Dreamhouse. The exercise focused on teaching the girls basic skills for drawing floor plans and encouraging them to explore their ideal domestic environment. (The workshop materials were later posted on the AIA website, and Architect Barbie workshops have since been held in locations as diverse as Ludwig Mies van der Rohe's Crown Hall on the Illinois Institute of Technology's campus in Chicago and the Navajo Nation Museum in Window Rock, Arizona.[24])

At the Morial Convention Center in New Orleans, the Mattel booth combined workshop and exhibition space. The latter included dolls from Barbie's previous careers in male-dominated professions spanning nearly fifty years, from Miss Astronaut Barbie (1965) to Computer Engineer Barbie (2010), and, of course, the newcomer, Architect Barbie. The A-frame Barbie Dreamhouse from 1979 was also on display alongside the contemporary townhouse model. The workshop area featured long white picnic tables with space for about thirty girls in total. Above the whole hung an enormous Barbie sign, like a hot-pink beacon. It is an understatement to say that in the cavernous expo hall, an overwhelmingly masculine landscape of companies selling everything from drain pipes to the latest building technologies, the Barbie booth and its young occupants stood out. We quickly became an expo attraction.

The girls, however, were oblivious to the attention. With a focus that surprised even us and that never wavered, the girls displayed an intense desire to learn how to shape and control their own spaces. Some of the girls admitted that before the workshop, they had not known women could be architects; with Barbie herself giving the go-ahead, they got to work with a vengeance. One of my favorite floor plans, created by a seven-year-old, included a room for monsters; acknowledging their presence and giving them their own space would allow the rest of the house to remain monster-free—a design solution to an eternal childhood problem that would have put Freud out of business. At the end of the workshop, each girl left with a gift bag that included drawing tools and her own Architect Barbie.

At no point during the workshops did I hear any girl question her spatial skills or the appropriateness of architecture

Where Are the Women Architects?

7. Girls participating in the Architect
Barbie workshops at the American
Institute of Architects Convention in
New Orleans, May 2011.

for women. And that, precisely, is where Barbie's power lies. The
fact is that Barbie appeals to little girls like no other toy. They are
proprietary about her—they know the doll is just for them. And
whatever Barbie does, she brings it into the sphere of women.
She has the power to make things seem natural to little girls.
Admittedly, Architect Barbie can't do all the heavy lifting. Deeply
held attitudes about women must shift before architecture
becomes a profession that truly embraces diversity. Open discussions about how to encourage and keep women in practice need
to happen in architecture schools, around the water cooler,
in boardrooms. If Architect Barbie gets us talking, then more
power to her. But ultimately she is for kids, not adults, and it is
the politics of the sandbox that I hope to influence. I look forward to the day when little girls claim hard hats and construction
sites as just another part of their everyday world.

Chapter 4

Architecture Prizes and the Boys' Club

When Zaha Hadid won the Pritzker Architecture Prize in 2004, not a single journalist failed to mention her gender. For the first time in its twenty-five-year history, the prestigious and highly coveted honor had been bestowed upon a woman. For some, Hadid's victory surpassed the personal or professional to represent a triumph for her gender. Architecture's highest and most lustrous glass ceiling had finally shattered. Or so it seemed.

Hadid received the typical press accolades for Pritzker Prize winners, her work labeled "bold," "radical," "visionary," and "genius."[1] Highly unusual for such coverage, however, were the less complimentary personal references, such as to Hadid's reputation for being "difficult" and a "diva," suggesting a female excess and instability of emotion.[2] Indeed, in some instances it would have been unthinkable for a journalist to write about a male laureate in a similar manner. For example, *Guardian* reporter Stuart Jeffries, who interviewed Hadid shortly after she won the prize, began his story with the following unflattering description: "Zaha Hadid offers a moist, limp hand to shake. She's coming down with the flu. This is a disappointment. Where is the vibrant monster I'd been promised from previous interviews? Where's the ball-breaking harridan barking abuse in Arabic into her mobile as she wafts into her north-London studio in vertiginous heels, before snarling unpleasant things to her staff in terrifyingly idiomatic Anglo-Saxon?" As Jeffries reported, the anticipated monster in heels, who looked at him with "sad brown eyes," was worn down from her nonstop travel following the prize announcement. Later in the article he raised the issue of "the C-word, one that only the boldest use

8. Zaha Hadid, the architect of the Riverside Museum in Glasgow, Scotland, pictured in front of that building on June 9, 2011. The transportation museum, Hadid's first major project in Britain, opened later that month. In 2013 it won the European Museum of the Year Award. Photograph by Jeff J. Mitchell, Getty Images News, Getty Images.

in Hadid's presence." He archly explained that he meant Hadid's controversial design for the Cardiff Bay Opera House, her 1994 winning competition entry that politicians, spurred by media opposition to the project, refused to construct. The article ended by describing Hadid as "workaholic and single . . . destined to have only one longtime companion—galloping influenza" as the price of her global travels and success.[3] Edwin Heathcote of the *Financial Times* also managed to put a negative spin on the prize. He raised the question—not the only journalist to do so— of whether Hadid's gender had helped her win and ended his interview with the architect by asking her whether she thought she deserved the prize. Hadid replied, "I don't know how to answer that . . . some people must think I deserve it."[4]

In an article published in the *New York Times* a few days after the prize announcement, architecture critic Herbert Muschamp took it upon himself to analyze what he considered Hadid's long-delayed entry "into the world of major big-time builders." In large measure, he blamed the architect herself: "She acquired the reputation for being difficult. And she looked the part. Some admirers began to fear that Hadid was investing more in her public image than in the discipline of professional practice." Muschamp contended that, for years following Hadid's graduation from the Architectural Association School in London, while others had profited from her ideas, "the lady herself, dazzling in Miyake, appeared content to stop traffic in Piccadilly with her astonishing physical appearance." But the failure of Cardiff, according to Muschamp, forced the architect to struggle with her self-defeating behavior: "Her lecture style changed. Her descriptions of projects became less fuzzy and erudite. . . . She began to show more appreciation toward her supporters. She became less keen to conceal the stress of disappointment and hard work. Gradually, another person emerged, a side of Hadid that resembles a big, raucous peasant woman. This strain is more pronounced than the intellectual side of her, in fact." Muschamp continued, "She is not someone you would talk to about books. Earthier appetites seem to drive her. I myself do not care greatly for lamb testicles. Should a sudden craving for this delicacy come over me, however, I would know whom to call."[5]

In reforming herself and becoming less neurotic, according to Muschamp, Hadid had turned from erudition (culturally coded as masculine) to the pleasures of the body (associated with the feminine). He informed readers, "You might find Hadid lying by the pool at the Delano in South Beach, where she often goes to chill out, her body glistening with oil, hands swatting at imaginary flies. She could almost be a British housewife letting her hair down at Butlin's Holiday Camps. And her laugh is a real ah-hah-hah!"[6]

Muschamp went on to argue that following Hadid's "relaxation of defenses," her architecture had also developed in a more "organic" manner. He compared her designs with those of leading male designers. Here, too, his interpretation was deeply influenced by Hadid's gender. Her plan for an expansion of the Price Tower Arts Center in Bartlesville, Oklahoma, for example, an art and architecture museum "now housed in Frank Lloyd Wright's only skyscraper, is to encircle the tower with another 55,000-square-foot structure. Rather than defer to Wright's building, Hadid's will 'flirt' with it—her sensuous, sinewy lines are designed to accentuate the tower's verticality." Muschamp thus orientalized Hadid's project, representing it as an architectural–sexual pairing between the sensual woman from the East and the phallic Western master.[7]

Robert Ivy, then editor-in-chief of *Architectural Record*, lambasted the demeaning press coverage of Hadid's achievement. "Can you imagine the leading practitioners in other professions treated to such personal scrutiny on receiving a major award? Marie Curie, for instance, subjected to fashion commentary. Or Nobel Laureate Toni Morrison appraised for her hairstyle. In receiving the Pritzker, Hadid joins those noble ranks and deserves better. Architecture deserves better." Ivy singled out Muschamp, criticizing his attention to "the quirks of [Hadid's] personality." In particular, he took issue with Muschamp's narrative of Hadid's maturation, asking, "Would male architects be subject to such amateur psychoanalysis?" Of the image of the well-oiled poolside Hadid, Ivy remarked, "Having learned what we did not care to know, regretfully we did not adequately learn why Hadid deserved the prize."[8]

Ivy's protest over the dismissive treatment accorded to Hadid, although directed at the media, recalled earlier criticism of the Pritzker judges. Indeed, the honor of being the first woman selected for the award had fallen to Hadid because of a previous— and, to some, grievous—omission. In 1991, the Pritzker jury had ignited a controversy when it awarded the prize to Robert Venturi without including his wife and partner, Denise Scott Brown, an architect, planner, and writer with whom he shared a firm as well as an active and close collaboration dating back three decades.[9] Although the official reason for the sole nomination was that the award honored individual architects and not part- nerships or firms, there was a precedent for giving two awards in one year: in 1988, Gordon Bunshaft and Oscar Niemeyer, independent of each other, had shared the prize. (A decade later, in 2001, the Pritzker ignored its own criteria in order to honor the male partnership of Jacques Herzog and Pierre de Meuron.) The laureate Venturi himself publicly deplored the lack of equal accreditation.[10] Without his partner, he stated in his acceptance speech, "there would be significantly less dimension within the scope and quality of the work this award is acknowledging today . . . and in the quality of our design where Denise's input, creative and critical, is crucial." Scott Brown chose not to attend the ceremony.[11] When asked about the omission by a *Los Angeles Times* reporter, she blamed an insecure profession that needed to create male superstars to lead the way. "You can't make a mom-and-pop-guru," she explained.[12]

Ironically, Scott Brown had been making the point about architecture's gendered star system, which the Pritzker exclu- sion only served to underscore, for a very long time. In 1974, she gave a talk at the West Coast Women's Design Conference in Oregon—published in 1989 as the influential essay "Room at the Top? Sexism and the Star System in Architecture"—

in which she described her struggles to be recognized as her husband's artistic collaborator or simply as an architect in her own right. She argued that critics (and award-givers, one might add) were invested in their role as "kingmaker for a particular group," which allowed them to share in the aura of the "few." She continued: "The kingmaker-critic is, of course, male; though he may write of the group as a group, he would be a poor fool in his eyes and theirs is he tried to crown the whole group king. There is even less psychic reward in crowning a female king." Despite Venturi's insistence on their firm's collaborative practice and his request for proper attribution of his partner's ideas and work, critics usually ignored Scott Brown or made "a pro forma attribution in an inconspicuous place"—an all-too-accurate description, one notes, of the cursory description of her contributions in the eleventh (and second-to-last) paragraph of the Pritzker announcement of her husband's prize: "Denise Scott Brown has been his collaborator in the evolution of architectural theory and design for the past 30 years. They have been married for 24 years. They have written two other books, *Learning from Las Vegas* (with Steven Izenour) and *A View from the Campidoglio: Selected Essays, 1953–1984*."[13]

As the stories of Hadid and Scott Brown show, the pairing of architecture prizes (or at least the big ones) and women raises hackles. Hadid won the Pritzker Prize amid talk that she did not deserve it; Scott Brown did not win the prize amid talk that she did not deserve it. The press reaction to Hadid's victory reveals an uncomfortable effort to position her in relation to the masculine mold of the star architect (eating or breaking balls, if not possessing them), whereas Scott Brown's exclusion suggests a more straightforward casting out (wives not admitted). No solo female architect has won the Pritzker Prize since Hadid, nor has a husband-and-wife architectural team ever been honored. In 2010, Kazuyo Sejima won the prize along with her younger male partner and SANAA (Sejima and Nishizawa and Associates) co-founder Ryue Nishizawa (the two are not a couple). The prize announcement praised their "unique and inspirational" collaborative method of working.[14] Yet the following year, the prize was won by Wang Shu and not his wife and architectural partner, Lu Wenyu, with whom he had founded an architectural practice fifteen years earlier (and with whom he had constructed thirteen of the fourteen projects cited in the Pritzker announcement), again prompting criticism of the jury.[15] Indeed, to date, of the thirty-nine Pritzker Prize laureates, only two (or about 5 percent) are women.

In the spring of 2013, the issue of women and architecture prizes exploded into public consciousness. It began in March with videotaped remarks made by Scott Brown to the *Architects' Journal*. Asked about the Pritzker, she was critical of the outmoded architectural values that had come to define the award. Of her own dismissal some two decades earlier, the now eighty-one-year-old architect felt it was time for a simple gesture of atonement. "They owe me not a Pritzker Prize but a Pritzker inclusion ceremony," she said. "Let's salute the notion of joint creativity." Rory Olcayto, then the journal's deputy editor, took up the call. "In 1991 there should have been two winners but instead there was only one," he wrote. "Is the Pritzker Prize bold enough to acknowledge past mistakes?"[16]

Two students at Harvard's Graduate School of Design, Arielle Assouline-Lichten and Caroline James, decided to press the issue. In late March, they created an online petition demanding that the Pritzker recognize Scott Brown for her contributions to the body of work honored by the 1991 prize. They chose as their venue Change.org, a social action platform with millions of members globally. The outpouring of support for Scott Brown was immediate and gained momentum as the weeks passed. By late May, more than twelve thousand people had signed, including nine Pritzker laureates, among them Zaha Hadid, Rem Koolhaas (who called Scott Brown's exclusion "an embarrassing injustice"), and Robert Venturi, who added, "Denise Scott Brown is my inspiring and equal partner."[17] The petition also garnered attention from leading news outlets, such as the *New York Times* and CNN. Under mounting pressure, Martha

The Pritzker Architecture Prize Committee: Recognize Denise Scott Brown for her work in Robert Venturi's 1991 Prize

9. Screenshot (detail) of the Denise Scott Brown petition posted on Change.org by Arielle Assouline-Lichten and Caroline James in the spring of 2013.

Thorne, the Pritzker's executive director, referred the request to the sitting jury.[18]

The media buzz about the petition also provoked negative and even hostile responses, encouraged by the Internet's cloaking anonymity. Detractors posting in the comments section of an article about the petition published in the online *Dezeen Magazine,* for example, portrayed Scott Brown as an overreaching wife or an ungrateful shrew. "I didn't know you could just ask for awards," wrote Colonel Pancake (who apparently did not know that 1988 winner Gordon Bunshaft had done just that, calling the Pritzker executive director and nominating himself).[19] When a poster pointed out that Scott Brown deserved recognition because her name, too, was on the firm's door, salvatore

10. Caroline James (left) and Arielle Assouline-Lichten by the entrance to Harvard's Graduate School of Design, 2013.

responded: "Her name is on the door because her husband put it there! And you and I know what he got in exchange. Without him she would be just another architect like thousands and thousands of others who don't deserve the Pritzker." Some posters objected to Scott Brown's "mak[ing] a fuss now," so long after the fact, and Frank speculated that "she is probably speaking up now that Robert Venturi is retired and probably mute."[20]

In June, Peter Palumbo, chair of the 2013 Pritzker jury, wrote to Assouline-Lichten and James to say that the jury could not

Where Are the Women Architects?

"second guess" the decision made by an earlier panel and that there would be no retroactive acknowledgment for Scott Brown. He conceded, however, "that certain recommendations or discussions relating to architectural creation are often a reflection of particular times or places, which may reflect cultural biases that underplay a woman's role in the creative process." But if, as this carefully worded statement seemed to imply, the 1991 jury had been guilty of an oversight, there was no suggestion of making amends. Instead, Palumbo noted that Scott Brown was still eligible to win a Pritzker, along with any other architect, implying that her work had not already done so.[21]

Despite the refusal, Assouline-Lichten and James, emboldened by more than eighteen thousand signatures, reiterated their determination "to set the record straight." They also insisted on the Pritzker's obligation to take a hard look at its practices: "Addressing these biases now is a moral and decent act to ensure that these injustices won't happen again."[22] Others, angered by Palumbo's dismissive tone and unwillingness to engage in a meaningful dialogue, called on past Pritzker Prize winners to renounce their awards.[23] Many felt the prize's luster had been tarnished, perhaps irrevocably. Kazys Varnelis, director of Columbia University's Network Architecture Lab, went even further: "I see no way in which we can, in good conscience, think of the Pritzker as being anything but a detriment to the profession."[24]

Yet, even if Scott Brown did not receive her desired inclusion ceremony, the petition—and the controversy it stirred—was anything but a failure. The mainstream media attention raised awareness about the many ways in which women in architecture, even at the top, suffer from ingrained prejudice. Moreover, in a profession with too few architectural heroines, "Scott Brown has become a role model not only for her revolutionary work in architecture, planning, and theory, but also for her perseverance and outspoken insistence on receiving credit where it is due."[25] More broadly, the petition provoked discussion about the collaborative nature of architectural practice and the need to give credit not only to women but also to the many key members of a team, who are overshadowed by the outmoded focus on a single star player. Some have suggested that organizations bestowing architecture prizes adopt an approach more like that of the Academy of Motion Picture Arts and Sciences, whose Oscars recognize the collective effort behind successful films.[26] Taking a step in the right direction, the AIA, prompted by the petition response and its own members, voted to make partnerships eligible for its highest honor, the Gold Medal.[27] With that revision, Venturi and Scott Brown became eligible to apply together; until then, their numerous joint submissions had always been rejected, and Venturi, in this instance, had refused to accept a lone nomination.[28] Finally, the petition had given something back to Scott Brown: "In a way my Pritzker Prize is the passion of all those people who responded to the petition and what they said. I am much less heart sore than I was."[29]

The Pritzker debate also brought attention to another neglected issue: the significance of architecture prizes. The twentieth century, particularly its last decades, witnessed the proliferation of such awards without much discussion about the values they promote. In the nineteenth century, there were only a handful of prizes to which an architecture student or practitioner might aspire. Among them, the Prix de Rome, created in 1720 by the French Royal Academy of Architecture, permitted the recipient to study for several years in Rome, enriching his (in its 248-year history, before the prize ceased in 1968, there were no female winners) knowledge of the classical tradition on which the academy's educational program was based. Today, as a glance at the Wikipedia page for architecture prizes reveals, there are dozens upon dozens of such prizes, some more financially valuable than the Pritzker. The Hyatt Foundation, which sponsors the Pritzker (named after the billionaire family that owns the hotel chain), has not increased the amount offered to laureates since it began awarding it in 1979—as Beverly Willis has pointed out, it nowhere nearly approximates the purse of the Nobel Prize, which the foundation claims as its model.[30] In the discussions surrounding the Scott

Brown controversy, many have wondered what, beyond money, such prizes are worth. Have they become obsolete? Does the Pritzker even matter?

From the point of view of individual career advancement, prizes can bring tremendous public recognition. As Alexandra Lange notes, after Wang Shu won the Pritzker in 2012, he made *Time*'s "100 Most Influential People in the World" list (his wife did not earn a mention).[31] They also have the power to confer legitimacy on winners and to get architects onto shortlists for prestigious projects.[32] Zaha Hadid has said that winning the Pritzker "does make a big difference in the way people treat you. They think your office can handle the work." Although the architect's designs were once considered strange and inaccessible, the prize shifted perceptions and opened up a new clientele. Her office enjoyed a surge of lucrative commercial building contracts as well as prestigious public commissions. Being placed in the rank of "world-class" architects meant that she made the lists of big names considered for such projects.[33]

In this sense, architecture prizes do matter, and the paucity of female laureates represents a real and tangible good denied women. Nor is the Pritzker the worst offender among architecture's loftiest awards. The Royal Gold Medal of the RIBA, created in 1848 and conferred to honor a lifetime of work, has gone to women only three times, and in each case there was an accompanying male partner. The Gold Medal of the AIA, founded in 1907, had never been awarded to a woman until 2014, when Julia Morgan, dead for five decades, won the prize thanks to an orchestrated campaign involving prominent women in architecture, journalism, and politics.[34] In total, if one combines the Pritzker Prize, the RIBA Gold Medal, and the AIA Gold Medal, there have been, until now, 281 winners, only 6 (or about 2 percent) of whom have been women.

But if prizes offer substantial individual benefits to the winners, some have asked what architecture itself gains as a profession. Bill Lacy, former executive director of the Pritzker Architecture Prize, insisted that the prizes did important work educating the public: "This may be the sort of publicity that creates celebrities, but there's such a lot of education to be done, and I think this coverage is healthy for the profession."[35] Others disagree, wondering whether perpetuating the myth of the "great man" damages the profession's image. As Mark Alden Branch writes, "Is the idea that architecture is about towering individual achievements by international celebrities the message we want to convey?" Moreover, the emphasis on form-making limits the definition of architecture. The most prestigious awards, Branch notes, are rarely given for architectural contributions to technology, the environment, or social justice.[36] Others have pointed the finger at the elite juries themselves, claiming that they are out of tune with the profession and its changing values and demographics. For this reason, the 2014 Pritzker Prize for Shigeru Ban's humanitarian designs was heralded as a "big deal" and a sign that the Scott Brown petition had shaken up the status quo. Indeed, Ned Cramer, writing in *Architect* magazine, suggested that the selection of Ban, while highly deserved, might also be "a calculated ploy, a grasp at political cover" to make amends and redeem the Pritzker's reputation.[37]

While waiting for the established big prizes in architecture to catch up with shifting ideals and practices, a number of organizations have instituted new types of awards that recognize contributions made to the profession by women or advancements in gender equity. Architecture thus joins other fields that are increasingly developing women-centered awards, borne out of frustration with the long neglect of female practitioners. In literature, for example, the Baileys Women's Prize for Fiction (formerly the Orange Prize) was created in response to the 1991 Booker Prize shortlist, which did not include a single female name.[38] The phenomenon in architecture is global and is proliferating rapidly. In the past few years, awards with a focus on women or gender equity in architecture have been instituted in the United States by *Architectural Record*, the University of California, Berkeley's College of Environmental Design, and the BWAF; in England by the *Architects' Journal*; in Italy by the Italcementi Group; and in Iraq by the Tamayouz Excellence Award.[39] On the whole, these prizes share the goal of celebrating the creativity of women in architecture and raising their profile in order to combat discrimination and provide role models. Most also have an explicitly social dimension, recognizing work that contributes to the greater public good. Thus the Berkeley-Rupp Prize, which is also open to men, is awarded to "a distinguished design practitioner or academic who has made a significant contribution to advance gender equity in the field of architecture, and whose work emphasizes a commitment to sustainability and community."[40] Some of these new prizes carry substantial monetary awards—the Berkeley-Rupp prize offers $100,000, the same amount as the Pritzker—which increases their desirability and underscores what some see as the waning relevance of the older elite prizes.

The creation of women-centered prizes has raised questions about the strategy of having separate awards. As Karen Burns asks, are prizes for women in architecture, which have been created to fight sexism, themselves sexist? And does the focus on individual practitioners replicate the star system? Burns acknowledges that "the relationship between the problem and the solution is messy." Nonetheless, she also views the establishment of women's prizes as "a provocative political act" that seeks to generate discussion and bring attention to prizes and their contexts, particularly "how reward systems work and who is rewarded." The new prizes may also benefit the winners through support for and public recognition of their work.[41]

A decade ago, the establishment of women-centered prizes would have been greeted with less openness by women in architecture. Until recently, many have objected to being labeled a "woman architect." But the recent outspokenness about discrimination in the profession has generated a newfound sense of solidarity and even pride in that identity. In 2012, Zaha Hadid was selected for the *Architects' Journal*'s inaugural Jane Drew Prize for "her outstanding contribution to the status of women in architecture." She was described by the judges as having "broken the glass ceiling more than anyone."[42] In an interview she gave to CNN after winning the award, Hadid remarked, "I used to not like being called a woman architect: I'm an architect, not just a woman architect." She continued, "Guys used to tap me on the head and say, 'You are okay for a girl.' But I see the incredible amount of need from other women for reassurance that it could be done, so I don't mind that at all."[43]

Chapter 5

Unforgetting Women Architects: A Confrontation with History and Wikipedia

History is not a simple meritocracy: it is a narrative of the past written and revised—or not written at all—by people with agendas. This is nothing new; about thirty-five hundred years ago, Thutmose III tried to erase the memory of his dead co-regent, Hatshepsut, one of Egypt's most successful pharaohs and prolific builders, in the most literal of ways: by hacking and scratching her name and image off of her monuments. His motives appear less passionate than political; he may have acted to protect his son, the future Amenhotep II, from rivals to the throne. Amenhotep II, in turn, seized the opportunity during his own reign to expand his legacy by claiming to be the creator of Hatshepsut's defaced works.[1] Many centuries later, such acts of erasure would become known as *damnatio memoriae* after the ancient Roman judgment passed on a person who was condemned not to be remembered. It was a dishonorable fate that the Roman Senate reserved for traitors and tyrants. Today, in modern architectural history, it is simply what we do to women architects.

The reasons we forget women architects are varied and complex. Until recently, historians assumed that there were no female practitioners before the mid-twentieth century, so they did not bother to look for them. Nor was it likely that they would stumble upon these designers by chance, given that traditional research methods focus on archives and libraries, institutions that have been slow to collect women's work. The International Archive of Women in Architecture, housed at Virginia Tech in

Blacksburg, was created in 1985 by Bulgarian architect Milka Bliznakov out of frustration at the enormous loss of material from the first generations of women architects.[2] Few archives wanted their papers, and as these women passed away, decades of drawings, plans, and records ended up in the trash. As a result, anyone seeking to learn about their lives and careers has had to be inventive and eclectic in the use of sources in order to supplement the archival documentation conventionally understood as the historian's primary materials.

Forgetting women architects has also been imbedded in the very models we use for writing architectural history. The monograph format, which has long dominated the field, lends itself to the celebration of the heroic "genius," typically a male figure defined by qualities such as boldness, independence, toughness, and vigor—all of which have been coded in Western culture as masculine traits.[3] Moreover, the monograph is usually conceived as a sort of genealogy, which places the architect in a lineage of "great men," laying out both the "masters" from whom he has descended and the impressive followers in his wake. For those seeking to write other kinds of narratives, the monograph has felt like an intellectual straitjacket, especially in contemplating the lives and careers of women that do not fit the prescribed contours.[4] Some of the early histories of women architects used the monographic model to produce a thin substratum of female "greats," but they did not thereby challenge the idea that the best architecture is created by mavericks. To be sure, in the past two decades, historians interested in broader, socially based histories have moved away from the monograph's confining format. But it remains powerful and continues to be the bible of the star system. Prominent architects seeking to consolidate their positions in history's pantheon often write or commission their own monographs, projects that are rarely self-critical.[5]

The monograph's insistence on heroic individualism has also discouraged histories about collaborations, as if acknowledging the work of a team would diminish the pot of glory. This has contributed significantly to the forgetting of women architects

Where Are the Women Architects?

because it is common for them to work in partnership (for professional and personal reasons), usually with a male who is often also a spouse. Even when a woman has been a full and equal partner, her contribution is rarely recognized as such.[6] The painful negation of Denise Scott Brown in the 1991 awarding of the Pritzker Prize solely to her husband and collaborator, Robert Venturi—which prompted the global petition on Change.org demanding that the Hyatt Foundation, twenty-two years later, set the record straight—is an important, but by no means exceptional, example of how female partners are written out of history by a profession suffering from star architect disorder (a.k.a. SAD).

Scott Brown's case is notable, however, not only because of the controversy it has generated but also because she has been an outspoken critic of her own erasure, bringing attention to the sexism of architecture's star system since long before the Pritzker Prize jury all but sealed her argument with their verdict.[7] But even when women architects have stood up for their own contributions, most historians and prize juries—following the cultural practice of glorifying individual heroes—have usually ignored them, no matter how compelling the evidence of their roles. Using pens rather than chisels, such historians and juries have channeled Thutmose III, removing the names of women architects from their own monuments.

Admittedly, women have sometimes enabled their own disappearance. Male architects do not hesitate to take an active role in preserving their legacies by writing memoirs and ensuring the safe-keeping of their models, drawings, and correspondence. Women—taught that self-promotion is an unattractive female trait—have made less effort to tell their stories. Among older generations, some women in partnerships have chosen to stand in the shadows in order to shine the spotlight on their husbands. Twenty years ago, I spent a day trying to interview a woman architect about her career, which had spanned thirty years, from 1948 to 1978. For the first six years, as a young graduate, she had worked together with her much older husband; after he died, in 1954, she had built a solo career. But every time

I asked about *her* projects, she would change the subject to her husband's achievements. After listening politely all morning, I finally told her that I wanted to hear about her contributions as well; she responded that I could only understand her through him (he had been her teacher before becoming her husband), and spent the afternoon telling me even more about her husband and her plans to write a book about him. We never did get around to talking about her work. It was an early lesson in frustration to a graduate student naively determined to rescue women architects from obscurity.

And yet, despite such hurdles, the past few decades have seen a remarkable florescence of books and articles on women architects. These writings have both contributed to and profited from the shift away from the monographic model as well as from increasing dialogue with other disciplines, such as anthropology and philosophy, which have introduced new narrative methods and sources. But although histories of women are now increasingly available, they have yet to become readily *visible*. They rarely appear in course syllabi; indeed, it is still common in architecture schools for students to complete an entire degree without ever having heard the names of women who practiced before 1970. You cannot walk into a large commercial bookstore, where the design shelves are filled with glossy monographs on international stars, and expect to walk out with a book on a woman architect. Their work is rarely exhibited in major museums, which have shown little interest in their careers or design legacies. In other words, there is a disconnect between the production of histories and their broader dissemination. The books and articles alone have not been enough to build a collective memory that recognizes women architects.

But there is something that we can all do to turn written words into public awareness. Namely, we can intervene to ensure the presence of women architects in online histories, which is increasingly important to do as the web becomes a primary site for making and preserving the cultural record. Their current scarcity in the virtual sphere threatens to reinforce the assumption among younger generations that women have not contributed significantly to the profession until very recently. The dearth of entries in the collectively produced free online encyclopedia Wikipedia, one of the most visited websites in the world, is particularly worrisome. But it is not just women architects who are missing. Although women comprise half of Wikipedia's readers, they are dramatically underrepresented among the ranks of the site's editors: only 9 percent of the site's editors were women in 2012, down from 13 percent in 2010. Not surprisingly, the gender gap among editors is reflected in a gender gap in content; male editors write about subjects with which they are familiar and that interest them.[8] Sue Gardner, then executive director of the Wikimedia Foundation, pledged to raise the number of women editors, while admitting that the website's culture resists female participation.[9] Women editors who submit new entries on women's history routinely find that male editors question their sources and the significance of their topics and are quick to nominate such entries for deletion. In a March 2012 edit-a-thon, "She Blinded Me with Science," held at the Smithsonian to add notable female scientists, entries were nominated for deletion almost as soon as they were posted.[10]

In 2013, I witnessed this kind of editorial hassling in action when someone tried to post about the architect Thekla Schild on the German Wikipedia site.[11] I had discovered Schild in the course of my dissertation research and had written about her efforts, in the years before the First World War, to integrate the architecture program of the Karlsruhe Institute of Technology. Schild's story is noteworthy not just because of her success in opening up the program to women (she was only the second woman in Germany to earn an architecture degree) but also because she wrote a memoir of the experience. Such firsthand accounts of academic integration are unusual in any field; in architecture, they are extremely rare. Schild's manuscript, which was never published, provides insights into what architectural education was like a century ago and how society viewed the status of architects.[12]

11. An image by Tom Morris encouraging women to embrace their editing power, March 2012. The image draws on the "We Can Do It!" poster created by J. Howard Miller in 1942 for the U.S. War Production Coordinating Committee as part of the World War II home-front mobilization campaign.

Given my prior interest, I noticed when, early in the morning of March 30, 2013, an editor with the user name CMdibev posted a brief entry on Schild. This editor, new to Wikipedia, had earlier in the same month posted numerous times on historical female figures, including on other women architects. Yet just thirteen minutes after the initial post on Schild appeared, a male editor, Der Krommodore, who has been posting on the site since 2008, had marked the article for immediate deletion (without the seven-day grace period for discussion usually afforded new entries). Admittedly, the entry on Schild seemed hastily written and was incomplete, and some of the criticisms were valid. But two things caught my eye (and raised my blood pressure): first, Der Krommodore asserted that Schild was not sufficiently accomplished to be listed on Wikipedia; and second, he expressed doubt that Schild *had ever existed*. During nearly twenty years of writing about women architects, I have certainly encountered dismissive attitudes toward the topic, but no one had ever denied the actual existence of my subjects. Der Krommodore, who identified himself as a Bavarian interested in linguistics as well as a monarchist and cigar-smoking, cognac-swilling insomniac, had Googled Schild and, finding nothing, assumed she was fictional. Eventually another editor told Der Krommodore to back off and give CMdibev time to complete the entry, but the latter seemed to give up. Over the next few weeks, however, other editors, in the kind of collaborative work that Wikipedia encourages, completed a detailed entry, thus saving Schild and baptizing her into the virtual world.

Still, the ease with which Der Krommodore could dismiss Schild was stunning—and this is exactly why ensuring the virtual presence of past women architects matters so much. As Mia Ridge, a young scholar and proponent of digital histories, argues, search engines are now shaping our conception of the world. A historian might spend decades undertaking research in archives and writing up discoveries in scholarly journals, but if the work does not have a presence online—and, specifically, a presence that is not behind a paywall—it is all but invisible outside academia.

12. Thekla Schild, encouraged by her mother, integrated the architecture program of the Karlsruhe Institute of Technology in 1908. Her memoirs describe what it felt like to walk into a packed, all-male lecture hall on her first day with the students and professor staring at her in astonishment.

Ridge puts the dilemma plainly: "If it's not Googleable, it doesn't exist."[13] And because Wikipedia articles usually show up first in Google search rankings, intervening on the site is especially important in establishing online visibility.

Just how much information and history is missing from Wikipedia becomes clear in comparison to the free, user-generated digital archive of American female architects created by the BWAF. The Dynamic National Archive, or DNA, includes over 1,100 practitioners from all fifty states, and it is still growing.[14] Wikipedia's "List of Female Architects," by comparison, includes in its U.S. category 114 female architects from some twenty-five states, but even these numbers are misleading because, of those 114 entries, 36, or a third, have no content at all (one links to the entry of a man with a similar name).[15] The DNA, too, has many entries that still need to be completed. Like Wikipedia, the BWAF relies on the public to build the database but also reaches out to experts to edit or to add entries. The BWAF is currently working on a National Endowment for the Arts–sponsored initiative, "Women of 20th-Century American Architecture," involving fifty scholars (I am one of them) who are researching and posting entries on fifty women chosen by a jury; this work will become part of its online collection. Although the BWAF archive does not rank as highly in Google searches as Wikipedia, some of the Wikipedia entries on American women architects cite it in their sources; adding more such links would increase the traffic between the sites.

The existence of female lists on Wikipedia arguably undermines the goal of integrating knowledge about women on the website. In April 2013, American novelist Amanda Filipacchi set off a fierce debate with her *New York Times* opinion piece about how Wikipedia's editors were quietly restructuring its categories to exclude women. "I just noticed something strange on Wikipedia," she wrote. "It appears that gradually, over time, editors have begun the process of moving women, one by one, alphabetically, from the 'American Novelists' category to the 'American Women Novelists' subcategory." The intention, she surmised, was to create an all-male "American Novelists" category.[16] As Joyce Carol Oates tweeted in response, "All (male) writers are writers; a (woman) writer is a woman writer." A few days later, technology author James Gleick, reporting on the growing controversy for the *New York Times Book Review* blog, noted that it was becoming apparent that the problem was broader and more pervasive than had first appeared. "Throughout Wikipedia, in all kinds of categories, women and people of nonwhite ethnicities are assigned only to their subcategories," he wrote. "Maya Angelou is in African-American writers, African-American women poets, and American women poets, but not American poets or American writers."[17]

Wikipedia's main "List of Architects," which spans the period from antiquity to the present, includes 755 architects. Of these, 726 are men and only 29 are women. Although male architects admittedly have had a larger presence in the field than women, the imbalance here is also the result of who participates in Wikipedia. Obscure male architects with few accomplishments are included, whereas one looks in vain for the names of more distinguished and influential female practitioners, such as Marion Mahony Griffin, Charlotte Perriand, Eileen Gray, Jeanne Gang, and others. Moreover, architectural practice is traditionally defined with a focus on the individual creator. Thus we find Robert Venturi listed under twentieth-century architects, but not Denise Scott Brown.[18]

I am not certain that the solution to the absence of women from the general "List of Architects" would be to simply merge that category with the "List of Female Architects," as was urged by many Wikipedians for "American Novelists" and the newly created subcategory "American Women Novelists" shortly after Filipacchi's piece appeared.[19] Wikipedia has many such lists concerning women, ranging from politicians in the United States Congress and CEOs of Fortune 500 companies to models on the *Price Is Right* television show. Not all of them are empowering, or meant to be. But there is something to be said for those cases, as with architecture, where women's contributions are so little known that a collection makes a point in and of itself—it visualizes a presence and a legacy, however hastily sketched out. At the same time, as Filipacchi points out, people "go to Wikipedia to get ideas for whom to hire, or honor, or read," and if they stumble first on the general page, as is most likely to happen, they may never realize that the women are missing.[20] For this reason, women will remain half-hidden if they appear solely on the "List of Female Architects."

The phenomenal attention garnered by the Scott Brown petition testifies not only to the power of the Internet and the support for her cause but also to a widespread dissatisfaction with the ongoing invisibility of women's accomplishments. In June 2013, when I first published an article in *Places Journal* on the threat of women architects' being yet again written out of history, now digitally, my call to action tapped into that discontent. Later that year, *East of Borneo*, an online art magazine based in Los Angeles, hosted the first edit-a-thon to write women architects into Wikipedia, citing my article and the Scott Brown petition controversy as their sources of inspiration.[21] In mid-May 2014, Arielle Assouline-Lichten, who, along with Caroline James, had instigated the petition, organized her own Wikipedia edit-a-thon at Storefront for Art and Architecture in New York City as part of a larger "Digital Invisibles" event devoted to increasing the online presence of marginalized histories in architecture.[22] Despite the pleasant weather and the lure of Central Park and other attractions that warm Saturday afternoon, eager would-be Wikipedians crowded the room.

Upholding the Internet's democratic potential, each of us can be a part of the effort to unforget a woman architect. Consider reading a book or an article on a woman architect and contributing what you have learned to the DNA (it is user-friendly, and there are no censorious Krommodores patrolling the premises) or to Wikipedia (numerous websites give tips on how to edit). Reach out to friends and colleagues with laptops and organize an edit-a-thon. And, if you are an educator, make Wikipedia-editing a class assignment.

13. Gearing up to write at the Wikipedia edit-a-thon organized by Arielle Assouline-Lichten and held on May 17, 2014, at the Storefront for Art and Architecture in New York City.

Contributing to Wikipedia and other online databases represents a real opportunity to provide students and younger readers as well as the larger public with a more accurate perception of women's participation in architecture. There is also something very satisfying about writing a forgotten figure—a professional ancestor, maybe even a pioneer—into history. And with each entry, the long and rich legacy of women in architecture grows brighter, making it that much harder to ignore women in architecture, whether in the classroom, in the museum, or on prize juries. As Sue Gardner of Wikimedia put it, "Wikipedia will only contain 'the sum of all human knowledge' if its editors are as diverse as the population itself: you can help make that happen. And I can't think of anything more important to do, than that."[23]

Where Are the Women Architects?

Looking Back, Moving Forward

Writing this book has sometimes felt like riding a bicycle with the winds of change blowing hard and fast on my back. After more than a century of the architectural profession's dodging its "woman question," it now seems that the equity debate— increasingly understood to affect practitioners of all genders— is everywhere, at least to those who are looking.

Almost as soon as she left the factory floor, Architect Barbie began to travel, an avid architectural tourist. On blogs, she has appeared at iconic sites of the "master" builders, including Buckminster Fuller's geodesic dome in Montreal and Frank Lloyd Wright's Taliesin in Spring Green, Wisconsin. At the University at Buffalo School of Architecture and Planning, a group of female students gave her a tour of the facilities, appropriating and transforming traditionally masculine areas, such as the machine and assembly shop.[1] Whether posing for a photograph or investigating architectural details, the doll has quietly gone about her business of grrrl interventions. She also continues to raise awareness about women in architecture with a broader audience—in recent years, Hallowe'en costumes have included a new couple: Bob the Builder and Architect Barbie.

On March 8, 2015, International Women's Day, ArchiteXX hosted a global Wikipedia edit-a-thon, "WikiD: Women Wikipedia Design," to increase the visibility of women architects on the website. The event, as described by Lori Brown, its chief organizer, took up my 2013 call to action in *Places Journal* but raised the scale of intervention to a whole new level.[2] Workshops were held in the United States, Australia, Germany, Canada, Ireland, Spain, and Portugal, with over seventy new entries created.

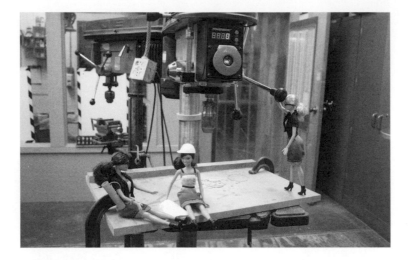

14. A team of Architect Barbies investigating the machine and assembly shop at the University at Buffalo School of Architecture and Planning in the spring of 2012. Photograph by Megan Basnak.

Brown reported that the workshop she supervised in New York City had unexpected teachable moments, including student volunteers' watching their entries being deleted by other Wikipedia editors minutes after they had been posted (without a grace period for discussion)—recalling similar experiences at the 2012 "She Blinded Me with Science" edit-a-thon, as noted in chapter 5. On the West Coast, archivists at UC Berkeley's Environmental Design Archives (EDA) participating in WikiD also reported numerous challenges to their entries, with Wikipedia editors questioning the significance of the women proposed and the resources used for references. When, after multiple drafts had been rejected, the pages were finally posted, some contained a disclaimer warning that the article was written in a way "that promotes the subject in a subjective manner without imparting

Where Are the Women Architects?

real information." As later noted by one of the archivists in *Tracings*, the EDA newsletter, she had been submitting entries for male architects, also based on materials from the archives, for two years without ever encountering the opposition and hurdles she and the others experienced with their entries on women architects.[3]

Nonetheless, WikiD's coordinated effort left its mark, and it attracted the attention of the profession's bloggers and media. It also brought to Wikipedia new editors interested in expanding our awareness of who builds; ultimately, enlarging this pool will have the greatest effect in redressing the website's gender imbalance on architectural subjects. Two months after the edit-a-thon, the Wikimedia Foundation recognized and supported its mission with a grant that will allow WikiD's organizers to establish a longer-term global partnership to continue the work of making women architects and professional equity issues visible online as well as to encourage more women in design to become active Wikipedia editors.[4]

Real-world venues for discussing women architects' status also continue to grow, suggesting the need for a different kind of community—one that is physically present—in voicing concerns and searching for solutions. Recent events focused on women in architecture held in Dallas, London, Los Angeles, Manchester, New York, and San Francisco all sold out, further testifying to the demand.[5] In November 2014, the Sam Fox School of Architecture held a symposium, "Women in Architecture," to mark the fortieth anniversary of a national event held there at the height of the women's movement. Like its predecessor in 1974, the conference was organized by female architecture students, and speakers included participants from the first event, thus uniting second- and third-wave feminists around the cause of professional equity. Hannah Roth, who, as a graduate student, had chaired the 1974 symposium, noted that although women had made substantial progress, "obstacles and institutional barriers still exist—and can be maddeningly difficult to uproot." Grace Davis, an undergraduate student organizer of the 2014 event, framed the symposium's conversations as "both retrospective and forward-thinking." Specifically, "How much has changed since 1974, and how do we see ourselves moving forward?" Although men represented a minority of the speakers and audience, their presence at the event attests to the concerns raised by this question among a growing cross-section of current and future architects.[6]

Despite the global support garnered by the 2013 Denise Scott Brown petition, its longer-term impact remains questionable in the insular world of establishment architecture prizes. The Pritzker Architecture Prize has not added a woman to its ranks since 2010. Of the current forty laureates, two are women, and Zaha Hadid remains the only woman to win without a male partner. Julia Morgan stands alone as the sole female winner of the AIA Gold Medal, which has yet to be awarded to a living female architect. Scott Brown, meanwhile, still awaits her inclusion ceremony.

The winds of change often blow back as resistance. In January 2015, the *Architects' Journal* published its latest "Women in Architecture" survey, which the editor himself admitted "makes for a depressing read." Some of the news is positive, including signs that the pay gap between male and female architects, although still pronounced, is slowly closing. At the same time, the report indicates that sexual discrimination is on the rise: 75 percent of female respondents report having experienced it during their architecture careers, up dramatically from 63 percent in the 2011 survey (although the journal acknowledged that the higher number may be due to greater awareness). And, contradicting stereotypes of "the leering scaffolder or the patronising project manager as the main offender," the journal noted that "most women said they were more likely to encounter discrimination in the office than on site." Moreover, the survey suggests that women architects are abandoning larger firms with a sense of defeat, believing that they will never be able to overcome those firms' rigid hierarchies and get ahead. Thus "progress," in terms of women architects' career strategies, appears to depend,

15. Pooja Bhatt, a University at Buffalo architecture graduate student, helping to construct the GRoW Home, the school's entry in the 2015 U.S. Department of Energy's Solar Decathlon, in May of that year. Photograph by Zhi Ting.

to a notable degree, on their opting out of large architecture firms, which are thus assured of remaining a bastion of financial rewards and prestigious, highly visible projects for men. (As Equity by Design has pointed out, salaries in large offices are significantly higher on average than those offered by small firms.[7]) Only half of the female respondents said they would encourage a woman to start a career in architecture today.[8]

Responses from men, who made up 20 percent of the 1,100 participants in the *Architects' Journal* survey, reveal a significantly different understanding of architecture's gendered working conditions. Eighty-two percent of male students stated that there are "as many opportunities for women as there are for men in architecture." A third of male practitioners asserted that they were not paid more than their female colleagues, while only

5 percent stated that they were; many chose to skip this question on the survey. It is perhaps not surprising that more men (62 percent) than women (48 percent) oppose salary transparency in their workplace.[9] This glimpse of the starkly different worlds inhabited by some male and female respondents underscores the need for even more studies, publications, workshops, symposia, protests, and other campaigns to raise awareness about the profession's entrenched gender disparities. Moreover, we need to ensure that the discussions thus provoked become not only more frequent and audible but also more inclusive. Even if it seems that we are talking more than ever about architecture's inequities, those truly engaged in the conversation remain a small minority of the profession.

Yet it is not just men who sometimes fail to realize how far architecture has to go before it can call itself an equal-opportunity profession. Recently a female architecture student approached me about undertaking a research project on the current status of women in the discipline. As she explained, because she and her female peers had not experienced discrimination in architecture school, she surmised that the barriers that had once confronted women architects now lay in the past or, at the very least, that "things are not that bad anymore." I understood that behind this premise of change lay both hopes and fears about the future before her, and I encouraged her to learn and be prepared. "Go ahead," I said, "and see what you find."

Notes

Chapter 1: May Women Practice Architecture? The First Century of Debate

1. "Women in Art," *American Builder and Journal of Art*, September 1, 1872, 52.
2. Ibid.
3. Paula Baker, "The Domestication of Politics: Women and American Political Society, 1780–1920," *American Historical Review* 89, no. 3 (1984): 620–47.
4. "The Woman Architect," *Washington Post*, September 26, 1880; "Women Architects," *Cincinnati Enquirer*, September 11, 1880; Margaret Hicks, "The Tenement-House Problem—II," *American Architect and Building News*, July 31, 1880. The assumption that women architects would practice domestic architecture was widespread. See, for example, Countryside, "Women Architects," *Arthur's Home Magazine* 53 (June 1885), 368; "Women as Architects," *British Architect*, January 5, 1900, 16–17; "What a Woman Architect Could Do," *Building Age*, January 1, 1911, 38. For a discussion of similar views in Germany, see Despina Stratigakos, "Architects in Skirts: The Public Image of Women Architects in Wilhelmine Germany," *Journal of Architectural Education* 55, no. 2 (2001): 96–98.
5. [Thomas Raggles Davison], "May Women Practise Architecture?" *British Architect*, February 21, 1902.
6. Karl Scheffler, *Die Frau und die Kunst* [Woman and art] (Berlin: Julius Bard, 1908), 40–42, 57, 95, 102. For more on Scheffler, see Stratigakos, "Architects in Skirts."
7. Karl Scheffler, "Vom Beruf und von den Aufgaben des modernen Architekten. Schluss" [On the profession and responsibilities of the modern architect: Conclusion], *Süddeutsche Bauzeitung* 19, no. 14 (1909): 110.
8. Karl Scheffler, "Vom Beruf und von den Aufgaben des modernen Architekten" [On the profession and responsibilities of the modern architect], *Süddeutsche Bauzeitung* 19, no. 13 (1909): 97, 99.
9. Ibid., 98; Scheffler, "Vom Beruf," *Süddeutsche Bauzeitung* 19, no. 14 (1909): 110.
10. Otto Bartning, "Sollen Damen bauen?" [Should ladies build?], *Die Welt der Frau (Gartenlaube)*, no. 40 (1911): 625–26.
11. Ayn Rand, *The Fountainhead* (New York: Signet, 1993), 216–17, 608–16.
12. Despina Stratigakos, "The Uncanny Architect: Fears of Lesbian Builders and Deviant Homes in Modern Germany," in *Negotiating Domesticity: Spatial Productions of Gender in Modern Architecture*, ed. Hilde Heynen and Gülsüm Baydar (London: Routledge, 2005), 145–61.
13. "Closet Wonders," *Sun* (Baltimore), June 11, 1911.
14. Lucile Erskine, "Woman in Architecture," *Cincinnati Enquirer*, October 8, 1911.
15. Jeanne Madeline Weimann, *The Fair Women* (Chicago: Academy Chicago, 1981), 141–80; Harriet Branton, "The Forgotten Lady Architect," *Observer-Reporter* (Washington, PA), April 23, 1983; "Successful Woman Architect," *Chicago Daily Tribune*, August 26, 1896; Despina Stratigakos, "Women and the Werkbund: Gender Politics and German Design Reform, 1907–14," *Journal of the Society of Architectural Historians* 62, no. 4 (2003): 490–511.

16. Stratigakos, "Women and the Werkbund," 506; Stratigakos, "The Uncanny Architect," 151.

17. Charlene G. Garfinkle, "Women at Work: The Design and Decoration of the Woman's Building at the 1893 World's Columbian Exposition" (Ph.D. diss., University of California, Santa Barbara, 1996), 56–57.

18. "These Girls Are Architects: Their Designs for a Hospital in San Francisco Have Been Accepted," *Chicago Daily Tribune*, December 15, 1894; "Planned by Two Women: Model Tenement-Houses to Be Built Soon in This City," *New York Tribune*, February 24, 1895.

19. Fritz Daussig, "Ein weiblicher Architekt" [A female architect], *Daheim* 45, no. 48 (1909): 14.

20. Lynne Walker, "Women Architects," in *A View from the Interior: Women and Design*, ed. Judy Attfield and Pat Kirkham (London: Women's Press, 1995), 99.

21. "Women Architects Win Chicago Prize: Best Plans for a Neighborhood," *New York Times*, March 6, 1915. On Mead and Schenk, see Sarah Allaback, *The First American Women Architects* (Urbana: University of Illinois Press, 2008), 135–37, 219.

22. "Shakespeare Memorial Design Explained by Woman Architect," *Christian Science Monitor*, January 6, 1928; "Woman Architect's Prize: Winning Design for New Shakespeare Memorial Theater," *Manchester Guardian*, January 6, 1928; Gillian Darley, "A Stage of Her Own," *Guardian*, January 29, 2011.

23. "Women as Architects," *British Architect*; Mary Marshall, "The Call of Architecture for Women Workers: Women Have to Be Housekeepers—Why Should Men Plan the House?," *New York Tribune*, August 3, 1912; "Women Architects," *Christian Science Monitor*, September 12, 1921; Helen Woodward, "The Woman Who Makes Good: Women as Architects," *Chicago Defender*, June 10, 1933; "Gropius Tells Lacks of Properly Built Homes," *Daily Boston Globe*, May 22, 1938; Aileen, "Wanted: Women Architects! To Do Away with Domestic Difficulties," *Irish Times*, February 18, 1939; Mary Lou Loper, "Wanted: More Women Architects," *Los Angeles Times*, November 11, 1960; Lulu Stoughton Beem, "Women in Architecture: A Plea Dating from 1884," *Inland Architect* 15 (December 1971): 6. See also note 25.

24. Judith Paine, "Pioneer Women Architects," in *Women in American Architecture: A Historic and Contemporary Perspective*, ed. Susana Torre (New York: Whitney Library of Design, 1977), 62; Louise Bethune, "Women and Architecture," *Inland Architect and News Record* 17, no. 2 (1891): 21.

25. "Women Should Design Houses," *Times Pictorial* (*Irish Times*), February 21, 1953; "Women Architects Needed," *Globe and Mail*, April 24, 1962; "A Little Imagination Could Improve Look of 'Suburbia,'" *Irish Times*, June 2, 1972.

26. Nancy Poore, "Woman Architect Cashes in on Design Talent," *Chicago Tribune*, March 13, 1966.

27. Ada Louise Huxtable, "The Last Profession to Be 'Liberated' by Women," *New York Times*, March 13, 1977.

28. "U. S. Women Architects Number 379, Count Shows," *Chicago Daily Tribune*, May 21, 1939; "Women Gain Slowly in Technical Fields," *New York Times*, January 17, 1949; Thomas W. Ennis, "Women Gain Role in Architecture: Profession Yields Slowly," *New York Times*, March 13, 1960; Barbara Gius, "Women Virtually Absent in Field of Architecture," *Los Angeles Times*, March 16, 1975; "Where Are the Women Architects?," *Modern Review*, September 1923, 355; D. X. Fenten, *Ms. Architect* (Philadelphia: Westminster, 1977), 11.

29. Rita Reif, "Fighting the System in the Male-Dominated Field of Architecture," *New York Times*, April 11, 1971.

30. Jane Holtz Kay, "Women Architects—A Liberated Elite?," *Boston Globe*, September 13, 1970.

31. Rita Reif, "Women Architects, Slow to Unite, Find They're Catching Up with Male Peers," *New York Times*, February 26, 1973.

32. Gabrielle Esperdy, "The Incredible True Adventures of the Architectress in America," *Places Journal*, September 2012, http://placesjournal.org/article/the -incredible-true-adventures-of-the-architectress-in-america, retrieved November 30, 2014; Judith Edelman, "Task Force on Women: The AIA Responds to a Growing Presence," in *Architecture: A Place for Women*, ed. Ellen Perry Berkeley and Matilda McQuaid (Washington, DC: Smithsonian Institution Press, 1989), 117–23.

33. Reif, "Women Architects, Slow to Unite"; Esperdy, "The Incredible True Adventures of the Architectress in America"; Susana Torre, "Women in Architecture and the New Feminism," in *Women in American Architecture*, ed. Torre, 157.

34. Leslie Kanes Weisman and Noel Phyllis Birkby, "The Women's School of Planning and Architecture," in *Learning Our Way: Essays in Feminist Education*, ed. Charlotte Bunch and Sandra Pollack (Trumansburg, NY: Crossing Press, 1983), 224–45; Leslie Kanes Weisman, "A Feminist Experiment: Learning from WSPA, Then and Now," in *Architecture: A Place for Women*, ed. Berkeley and McQuaid, 125–33.

35. *Proceedings of the West Coast Women's Design Conference, April 18–20, 1974, University of Oregon* (n.p.: West Coast Women's Design Conference, 1975).

36. Ellen Perry Berkeley, "Women in Architecture," *Architectural Forum*, September 1972, 46–53; Esperdy, "The Incredible True Adventures of the Architectress in America."

37. Marita O'Hare, "Foreword," in *Women in American Architecture*, ed. Torre, 6–7; Susana Torre, "Introduction: A Parallel History," in *Women in American Architecture*, ed. Torre, 10–13; Rosalie Genevro and Anne Rieselbach, "A Conversation with Susana Torre," Architectural League of New York Web Feature, *Women in American Architecture: 1977 and Today*, http://archleague.org/2013/09/susana-torre, retrieved November 30, 2014.

38. Fenten, *Ms. Architect*.

39. See, for example, Inge Schaefer Horton, *Early Women Architects of the San Francisco Bay Area: The Lives and Work of Fifty Professionals, 1890–1951* (Jefferson, NC: McFarland: 2010); Despina Stratigakos, *A Women's Berlin* (Minneapolis: University of Minnesota Press, 2008); Ute Maasberg and Regina Prinz, *Die Neuen kommen! Weibliche Avantgarde in der Architektur der zwanziger Jahre* [Here come the new ones! Female avantgardists in 1920s architecture] (Hamburg: Junius, 2004); Julie Willis and Bronwyn Hanna, *Women Architects in Australia, 1900–1950* (Red Hill, Australia: Royal Australian Institute of Architects, 2001); Annmarie Adams and Peta Tancred, *"Designing Women": Gender and the Architectural Profession* (Toronto: University of Toronto Press, 2000); Renja Suominen-Kokkonen, *The Fringe of a Profession: Women as Architects in Finland from the 1890s to the 1950s* (Helsinki, 1992).

Chapter 2: The Sad State of Gender Equity in the Architectural Profession

1. National Architectural Accrediting Board, *2014 Annual Report from the National Architectural Accrediting Board, Inc., Part I: Programs, Students, and Degrees* (Washington, DC: National Architectural Accrediting Board, 2015), 11; Jane Duncan, "Why Are So Many Women Leaving Architecture," *Guardian*, August 7, 2013, http://www .theguardian.com/women-in-leadership/2013/aug/07/women-leaving-architecture -profession, retrieved December 20, 2014.

2. Josephine Bonomo, "Architecture Is Luring Women," *New York Times*, April 2, 1977.

3. Ellen Perry Berkeley, "Women in Architecture," *Architectural Forum*, September 1972, 47; Paul Goldberger, "Women Architects Building Influence in a Profession That Is 98.8% Male, *New York Times*, May 18, 1974; Ellen Futterman, "Women in Architecture: 100 Years and Counting," *St. Louis Post-Dispatch*, May 7, 1989; Kathryn H. Anthony, *Designing for Diversity: Gender, Race, and Ethnicity in the Architectural Profession* (Urbana: University of Illinois Press, 2001), 12–13; Cathy Simon, "Women in Architecture: What Are We Doing Here?," *Contract* 45, no. 3 (2003): 94.

4. Berkeley, "Women in Architecture," 48.

5. Graham Fraser, "Architecture Students Abused, Report Says: Teaching Environment at Carleton School Called Discriminatory, Unprofessional, Sexist," *Globe and Mail*, December 23, 1992; Anthony, *Designing for Diversity*, 19.

6. Laura Mark, "Bullying on the Rise in Architecture School," *Architects' Journal*, January 10, 2014, https://www.architectsjournal.co.uk/home/events/wia/bullying-on -the-rise-in-architecture-school/8657351.article, retrieved May 23, 2015.

7. See, for example, Matrix, *Making Space: Women and the Man Made Environment* (London: Pluto, 1984); American Architectural Foundation, *"That Exceptional One": Women in American Architecture, 1888–1988* (Washington, DC: American Architectural Foundation, 1988); Renja Suominen-Kokkonen, *The Fringe of a Profession: Women as Architects in Finland from the 1890s to the 1950s* (Helsinki, 1992); Leslie Kanes Weisman, *Discrimination by Design: A Feminist Critique of the Man-Made Environment* (Urbana: University of Illinois Press, 1992); Clara H. Greed, *Women and Planning: Creating Gendered Realities* (London: Routledge, 1994); Francesca Hughes, ed., *The Architect: Reconstructing Her Practice* (Cambridge, MA: MIT Press, 1998); Helen Searing et al., *Equal Partners: Men and Women Principals in Contemporary Architectural Practice* (Northampton, MA: Smith College Museum of Art, 1998); Annmarie Adams and Peta Tancred, *"Designing Women": Gender and the Architectural Profession* (Toronto: University of Toronto Press, 2000); Anthony, *Designing for Diversity*; Julie Willis and Bronywyn Hanna, *Women Architects in Australia, 1900–1950* (Red Hill, Australia: Royal Australian Institute of Architects, 2001); Sarah Allaback, *The First American Women Architects* (Urbana: University of Illinois Press, 2008); Despina Stratigakos, *A Women's Berlin* (Minneapolis: University of Minnesota Press, 2008); Inge Schaefer Horton, *Early Women Architects of the San Francisco Bay Area: The Lives and Work of Fifty Professionals, 1890–1951* (Jefferson, NC: McFarland: 2010).

8. Margit Kennedy, "Seven Hypotheses on Female and Male Principles in Architecture," *Making Room: Women and Architecture*, special issue, *Heresies* 3, no. 3, issue 11 (1981): 12–13; Phyllis Birkby, "Herspace," *Making Room: Women and Architecture*, special issue, *Heresies* 3, no. 3, issue 11 (1981): 28–29; Mimi Lobell, "The Buried Treasure: Women's Ancient Architectural Heritage," in *Architecture: A Place for Women*, ed. Ellen Perry Berkeley and Matilda McQuaid (Washington, DC: Smithsonian Institution Press, 1989), 139–57; Oliver Wainwright, "Zaha Hadid's Sport Stadiums: 'Too Big, Too Expensive, Too Much Like a Vagina,'" *Guardian*, November 28, 2013, http://www.theguardian.com /artanddesign/2013/nov/28/zaha-hadid-stadiums-vagina, retrieved December 3, 2014.

9. See, for example, Beatriz Colomina, ed., *Sexuality and Space* (New York: Princeton Architectural Press, 1992); Diana Agrest, *Architecture from Without: Theoretical Framings for a Critical Practice* (Cambridge, MA: MIT Press, 1993); Jennifer Bloomer, ed., *Architecture and the Feminine: Mop-Up Work*, special issue, *Any*, January/February 1994. For a critique of the exclusion of this feminist theory in subsequent architectural theory anthologies, see Karen Burns, "A Girl's Own Adventure: Gender in Contemporary Architectural Theory Anthology," *Journal of Architectural Education* 65, no. 2 (2012): 125–34.

10. Karen Kingsly, "Rethinking Architectural History from a Gender Perspective," in *Voices in Architectural Education: Cultural Politics and Pedagogy*, ed. Thomas A. Dutton (New York: Bergin and Garvey, 1991), 249–64; Diane Ghirardo, "Cherchez la femme: Where Are the Women in Architectural Studies?," in *Desiring Practices: Architecture, Gender and the Interdisciplinary*, ed. Katerina Rüedi, Sarah Wigglesworth, and Duncan McCorquodale (London: Black Dog, 1996), 156–73.

11. Mark, "Bullying on the Rise."

12. National Architectural Accrediting Board, *2014 Annual Report from the National Architectural Accrediting Board, Inc., Part III: Faculty* (Washington, DC: National Architectural Accrediting Board, 2015), 5.

13. Linda N. Groat and Sherry B. Ahrentzen, "Voices for Change in Architectural Education: Seven Facets of Transformation from the Perspectives of Faculty Women,"

Where Are the Women Architects?

Journal of Architectural Education 50, no. 4 (1997): 272, 277–79. Groat and Ahrentzen point out that the predominance of male faculty in upper-level design studios is not simply an outcome of the higher percentages of tenured male design faculty but also has to do with gendered perceptions that female faculty, including those in senior positions, are better suited to undertake the "nurturing" work of entry-level studios.

14. Lori Brown and Nina Freedman, "Women in Architecture: Statistics for the Academy," *Indigogo*, https://www.indiegogo.com/projects/women-in-architecture, retrieved December 20, 2014.

15. Mark, "Bullying on the Rise."

16. Anthony, *Designing for Diversity*, 12; National Architectural Accrediting Board, *2014 Annual Report from the National Architectural Accrediting Board, Inc., Part I*, 19; Alice Lipowicz, "Architects Make Gains, but Few Elevated to Top," *Crain's New York Business* 17, no. 25 (2001): 32; Stefanos Chen, "In Architecture, a Glass Ceiling," *Wall Street Journal* online, August 21, 2014, http://www.wsj.com/articles/in-architecture-a-glass-ceiling-1408633998, retrieved December 20, 2014.

17. Laura Mark, "88% Women Say Having Children Puts Them at a Disadvantage," *Architects' Journal*, January 10, 2014, https://www.architectsjournal.co.uk/home/events/wia/88-women-say-having-children-puts-them-at-disadvantage/8657348.article, retrieved May 23, 2015.

18. Ibid. See also Despina Stratigakos, "The Good Architect and the Bad Parent: On the Formation and Disruption of a Canonical Image," *Journal of Architecture* 13, no. 3 (2008): 283–96.

19. Anne Richardson, "Half the Mothers I Know Have Been Driven from Their Jobs," *Guardian*, August 8, 2013, http://www.theguardian.com/money/2013/aug/08/workplace-discrimination-pregnant-women-mothers-common, retrieved December 21, 2014; Ann de Graft-Johnson, Sandra Manley, and Clara Greed, *Why Do Women Leave Architecture?* (Bristol: University of the West of England–Bristol, and London: Royal Institute of British Architects, 2003), 17, 19; Mark, "88% Women Say Having Children Puts Them at a Disadvantage."

20. Mark, "88% Women Say Having Children Puts Them at a Disadvantage."

21. Ernest Beck, "Making the Mold: The Lack of Diversity in Architecture Isn't a Simple Problem, but There Are Better and Worse Ways to Approach the Issue," *Architect*, July 2, 2012, http://www.architectmagazine.com/practice/best-practices/making-progress-with-diversity-in-architecture_o, retrieved December 20, 2014.

22. AIA San Francisco and Equity by Design Committee, *Equity by Design: Knowledge, Discussion, Action! 2014 Equity in Architecture Survey Report and Key Outcomes*, report prepared by Annelise Pitts, Rosa Sheng, Eirik Evenhouse, and Ruohnan Hu (San Francisco: AIA San Francisco, 2015), 22 ff.

23. Ibid., 19, 21, 33; Laura Mark, "Gender Pay Gap Worst in America," *Architects' Journal*, January 10, 2014, http://www.architectsjournal.co.uk/home/events/wia/gender-pay-gap-worst-in-america/8657355.article, retrieved April 6, 2015; Laura Mark, "Pay Gap Widens: Women Architects Earn Less than Men," *Architects' Journal*, January 10, 2014, https://www.architectsjournal.co.uk/home/events/wia/pay-gap-widens-women-architects-earn-less-than-men/8657346.article, retrieved April 6, 2015; U.S. Bureau of Labor Statistics, "Household Data Annual Averages," 2014 (these figures include architects and engineers), http://www.bls.gov/cps/cpsaat39.pdf, retrieved April 6, 2015; de Graft-Johnson, Manley, and Greed, *Why Do Women Leave Architecture?*, 17.

24. American Institute of Architects, "Women in Architecture Toolkit," October 2013, 5, http://issuu.com/aiadiv/docs/women_in_architecture_toolkit, retrieved December 3, 2014; Eric Willis, "Five Firm Changes," *Architect*, October 2014, 122.

25. It is possible that an architect working toward licensure does so unofficially under a female supervisor, who does not have the authority to sign off as the National Council of Architectural Registration Boards (NCARB) supervisor. Even so, the degree of gender disparity in these figures leaves little doubt that male supervisors remain by far the dominant presence. National Council of Architectural Registration Boards, *2014 NCARB by the Numbers* (Washington, DC: National Council of Architectural Registration Boards, 2014), 6, http://www.ncarb.org/About-NCARB/~/media/Files/PDF/Special-Paper/NCARB_by_the_Numbers_2014.ashx, retrieved December 21, 2014.

26. Diana Griffiths, "A Lost Legacy," *Archiparlour*, April 18, 2012, http://archiparlour.org/authors/diana-griffiths, retrieved December 12, 2014; Sandra Kaji-O'Grady, "Does Motherhood + Architecture = No Career?," *ArchitectureAU*, November 20, 2014, http://architectureau.com/articles/does-motherhood-architecture-no-career, retrieved January 20, 2015.

27. Justine Clark, "Six Myths about Women and Architecture," *Archiparlour*, September 6, 2014, http://archiparlour.org/six-myths-about-women-and-architecture, retrieved December 12, 2014; de Graft-Johnson, Manley, and Greed, *Why Do Women Leave Architecture?*, 19.

28. Denise Scott Brown, "Room at the Top: Sexism and the Star System in Architecture," in *Architecture: A Place for Women*, ed. Berkeley and McQuaid, 245.

29. Lamar Anderson, "How Women Are Climbing Architecture's Career Ladder," *Curbed*, March 17, 2014, http://curbed.com/archives/2014/03/17/how-women-are-climbing-architectures-career-ladder.php, retrieved December 14, 2014; Anthony, *Designing for Diversity*, 166–67; Sheryl Sandberg, *Lean In: Women, Work, and the Will to Lead* (New York: Knopf, 2013), 66–67, 71.

30. Sandberg, *Lean In*, 65, 68.

31. Richard Waite and Ann-Marie Corvin, "Shock Survey Results as the AJ Launches Campaign to Raise Women Architects' Status," *Architects' Journal*, January 16, 2012, http://www.architectsjournal.co.uk/news/daily-news/shock-survey-results-as-the-aj-launches-campaign-to-raise-women-architects-status/8624748.article, retrieved December 21, 2014; Harriet Minter, "Sexism in Architecture: On the Rise," *Guardian*, January 13, 2014, http://www.theguardian.com/women-in-leadership/2014/jan/13/women-in-architecture-sexism, retrieved December 15, 2014; Laura Mark, "Sexual Discrimination on the Rise for Women in Architecture," *Architects' Journal*, January 10, 2014, https://www.architectsjournal.co.uk/home/events/wia/sexual-discrimination-on-the-rise-for-women-in-architecture/8657345.article, retrieved April 6, 2015.

32. Laura Mark, "Survey Shows Shocking Lack of Respect for Women Architects," *Architects' Journal*, January 10, 2014, https://www.architectsjournal.co.uk/survey-shows-shocking-lack-of-respect-for-women-architects/8657343.article, retrieved April 6, 2015.

33. Clark, "Six Myths about Women and Architecture"; de Graft-Johnson, Manley, and Greed, *Why Do Women Leave Architecture?*, 21. See also Karen Burns, "The Elephant in Our Parlour: Everyday Sexism in Architecture," *Archiparlour*, August 20, 2014, http://archiparlour.org/the-elephant-in-our-parlour-everyday-sexism-in-architecture, retrieved December 14, 2014.

34. Mabel Brown, "Women in Profession: VII—Architecture," *San Francisco Chronicle*, September 24, 1905.

35. "Architecture as a Profession for Women," *Journal of the Society of Architects* 5, no. 53 (March 1912), 188–89.

36. Brown, "Women in Profession."

37. "Why Not Women Architects? Great Demand and No Supply," *Journal of the Society of Architects* 6, no. 70 (August 1913): 393–94.

38. Mark, "Sexual Discrimination on the Rise for Women in Architecture."

39. Laura Mark, "Gender Pay Gap: 'Beyond Shocking,'" *Architects' Journal*, May 2, 2014, http://www.architectsjournal.co.uk/news/gender-pay-gap-beyond-shocking/8662077.article, retrieved April 6, 2015.

40. Beverly Willis Architecture Foundation, "Industry Leaders Roundtable Program," http://bwaf.org/roundtable/roundtable-about, retrieved December 15, 2014.

41. AIA San Francisco and Equity by Design Committee, *Equity by Design*, 36.

42. Sophia Saravamartha Meisels, "Half of Greek Architects Are Women," *Jerusalem Post*, December 24, 1967; Mizra and Nacey Research, *The Architectural Profession in Europe, 2014: A Sector Study Commissioned by the Architects' Council of Europe* (Brussels: Architects' Council of Europe, 2015), http://www.ace-cae.eu/fileadmin/New_Upload/7._Publications/Sector_Study/2014/EN/2014_EN_FULL.pdf, retrieved April 3, 2015.

43. Josh Mitchell, "Women Notch Progress: Females Now Constitute One-Third of Nation's Ranks of Doctors and Lawyers," *Wall Street Journal*, December 4, 2012; Philip Cohen, "More Women Are Doctors and Lawyers than Ever—but Progress Is Stalling," *Atlantic*, December 11, 2012, http://www.theatlantic.com/sexes/archive/2012/12/more-women-are-doctors-and-lawyers-than-ever-but-progress-is-stalling/266115, retrieved December 21, 2014. Cohen points out, however, that attrition—although at lower rates than in architecture—also exists in medicine and is slowing the progress toward parity.

44. For examples of promising work comparing architecture with other fields, see Adams and Tancred, *"Designing Women,"* and Anthony, *Designing for Diversity*.

45. American Institute of Architects, "Resolution 15–1, Equity in Architecture," *2015 AIA National Convention and Design Exposition: Official Delegate Information Booklet* (Washington, DC: American Institute of Architects, 2015), 15–16; Rosa Sheng, "Equity by Design: AtlAIAnta! Convention Recap," *Equity by Design: Missing 32 Percent Blog*, May 17, 2015, http://thomissing32percent.com/blog/2015/5/17/equity-by-design-aia-convention-atlanta-recap, retrieved May 23, 2015.

Chapter 3: What I Learned from Architect Barbie

1. Jodi S. Cohen, "Ground Zero of Affirmative Action Issue: As Michigan Voters Decide Whether Gender, Race Should Be Factors in Jobs and Admissions, the Outcome Could Affect the National Debate," *Chicago Tribune*, October 19, 2006; Peter Schmidt, "Michigan Overwhelmingly Adopts Ban on Affirmative-Action Preferences," *Chronicle of Higher Education*, November 17, 2006, A23–A24. This chapter draws on and expands an earlier article: Despina Stratigakos, "What I Learned from Architect Barbie," *Places Journal*, June 2011, http://places.designobserver.com/feature/what-i-learned-from-architect-barbie/27630, retrieved May 23, 2015.

2. Gabrielle Esperdy, "The Incredible True Adventures of the Architectress in America," *Places Journal*, September 2012, http://placesjournal.org/article/the-incredible-true-adventures-of-the-architectress-in-america, retrieved November 30, 2014. See also chapter 1.

3. Despina Stratigakos, "The Good Architect and the Bad Parent: On the Formation and Disruption of a Canonical Image," *Journal of Architecture* 13, no. 3 (2008): 283–96; *One Fine Day*, directed by Michael Hoffman, 1996 (Los Angeles, CA: 20th Century Fox, 2003), DVD; *Click*, directed by Frank Coraci, 2006 (Culver City, CA: Columbia Pictures Corporation, 2006), DVD.

4. Guerrilla Girls, *The Guerrilla Girls' Bedside Companion to the History of Western Art* (New York: Penguin, 1998).

5. Judy Schriener, "Architect Barbie in the Offing?" *Construction*, December 5, 2002, http://www.construction.com/NewsCenter/it/archive/20021205apf.asp, last accessed August 7, 2013. Site no longer working.

6. Stephen T. Watson, "Professor Builds Case for Barbie as Architect," *Buffalo News*, February 7, 2010; Melissa Harris, "Mattel Launching Computer Engineer Barbie: Society of Women Engineers CEO Helps Design New Career Doll," *Chicago Tribune*, April 14, 2010.

7. Despina Stratigakos, "Architects in Skirts: The Public Image of Women Architects in Wilhelmine Germany," *Journal of Architectural Education* 55, no. 2 (2001): 92–93.

8. Stefani Yocky, e-mail to the author and others, November 18, 2011.

9. Jonathan Glancey, "The Best Architecture of 2011: Jonathan Glancey's Choice," *Guardian*, December 5, 2011; Anna Winston, "The Top 10 News Stories of 2011," *BDonline*, December 30, 2011, http://www.bdonline.co.uk/the-top-10-news-stories -of-2011/5029650.article, retrieved January 30, 2015; Jaime Derringer, "Top 10 of 2011: Design," *USA Character Approved Blog*, December 7, 2011, http://www.characterblog .com/design/top-10-of-2011-design, retrieved May 30, 2013; Miguel Bustillo, "Search Is On for Hot Stuff," *Wall Street Journal*, December 8, 2011.

10. *Women in Practice*, special issue, *Architects' Journal*, January 12, 2012, cover; "What We Love," *Elle Decor*, July–August 2011, 30; Ella Alexander, "Architect Barbie," *Vogue* (U.K.), March 1, 2011, http://www.vogue.co.uk/news/2011/03/01/barbie-the -architect-launches, retrieved January 30, 2015.

11. Margaret Hartmann, "New Architect Barbie Designs Her Own Dream House," *Jezebel*, February 22, 2011, http://jezebel.com/5766877/new-architect-barbie- designs-her-own-dream-house, retrieved January 27, 2015.

12. "Architect Barbie," *indesignlive*, February 24, 2011, http://www.indesignlive.com/ articles/in-review/architect-barbie, retrieved March 20, 2011. The comments no longer appear on the archived page.

13. Sarah, comment made on February 18, 2011 (4:04) on Nancy Levinson, "Architect Barbie," *Design Observer*, February 18, 2011, http://designobserver.com/feature /architect-barbie/24718, retrieved January 25, 2015.

14. Sherrie A. Innis, "Barbie Gets a Bum Rap: Barbie's Place in the World of Dolls," in *The Barbie Chronicles: A Living Doll Turns Forty*, ed. Yona Zeldis McDonough (New York: Touchstone, 1999), 178–79; Anna Quindlen, "Barbie at 35," in *The Barbie Chronicles*, ed. McDonough, 119.

15. Peggy Orenstein, *Cinderella Ate My Daughter: Dispatches from the Front Lines of the New Girlie-Girl Culture* (New York: HarperCollins, 2011), 33 ff.

16. Jessica Lane, "The Audacity of Architect Barbie," *EHDD*, March 3, 2011, http:// www.ehdd.com/4440, retrieved January 30, 2015; Luke Butcher, "Architect Barbie," *Luke Butcher Blog*, April 6, 2011, http://lukebutcher.blogspot.com/2011/04/architect -barbie.html, retrieved January 30, 2015; siddharth lalka, comment made on February 22, 2011 (3:58 p.m.) on Anna Winston, "Mattel Reveals Architect Barbie," *BDonline*, February 21, 2011, http://www.bdonline.co.uk/mattel-reveals-architect-barbie /5013692.article, retrieved January 30, 2015.

17. Alissa Walker, "Architecture Is Tough! Will Architect Barbie Help More Women Become Designers?," *Good.is*, March 3, 2011, http://magazine.good.is/articles/ architecture-is-tough-will-architect-barbie-help-more-women-become-designers, retrieved January 30, 2012; Jerri Holan, "Architect Barbie: Role Model or Ridiculous?," *UrbDeZine San Francisco*, November 30, 2011, http://sanfrancisco.urbdezine .com/2011/11/30/architect-barbie-role-model-or-ridiculous, retrieved January 30, 2015; Karen Hewitt, "Does Architect Barbie Play with Blocks?," *Learning Materials Workshop Blog*, February 22, 2011, http://learningmaterialswork.com/blog/2011/02 /does-architect-barbie-play-with-blocks, retrieved January 30, 2015; Alexandra Lange, "Girl Talk," *Dwell*, July–August 2012, 92–94.

18. I have abridged the comments quoted here for the sake of readability and have also identified the posters by first names only. Inda, Adriana, Leslie, and Laura, comments on "Fetish in Pink," *American Institute of Architects LinkedIn Forum*, March–June 2011, http://www.linkedin.com/groupItem?view=&srchtype=discussedNews&gid=113822&item =45564786&type=member&trk=eml-anet_dig-b_pd-ttl-cn, retrieved June 17, 2011.

19. Tracey, Patricia, Ellie, comments on Levinson, "Architect Barbie."

20. "'Ladies (and Gents) Who Lunch with Architect Barbie' Event," October 13, 2011, *ArchDaily*, http://www.archdaily.com/?p=175512, retrieved January 30, 2015.

21. Lisa Boquiren, "What Can a Toy Do for Architecture?," *Metropolis*, November 2011, http://www.metropolismag.com/Point-of-View/November-2011/What-can-a

Where Are the Women Architects?

-toy-do-for-architecture, retrieved January 30, 2015.

22. "Origins," *Equity by Design: The Missing 32% Project*, http://themissing32percent.com/origins, retrieved January 30, 2015.

23. Lisa Boquiren, "In Equality—Architect Barbie's Journey to the Pritzker," *Metropolis*, July 9, 2013, http://www.metropolismag.com/Point-of-View/July-2013/In-equality-Architect-Barbies-Journey-to-the-Pritzker, retrieved January 30, 2015.

24. Lauren Finch, "Dreaming of the Future: AIA Chicago Joins CPS [Chicago Public Schools] for Inaugural Barbie Architect Workshop," *Chicago Architect*, January/February 2013, http://mydigimag.rrd.com/article/Dreaming_of_the_Future/1275362/140831/article.html, retrieved January 30, 2015; Yvette Morris, "Q&A with Tamarah Begay, AIA: Navajo Nation Architect, Barbie Ambassador," *AIArchitect*, August 23, 2013, http://www.aia.org/practicing/AIAB099854, retrieved January 30, 2015.

Chapter 4: Architecture Prizes and the Boys' Club

1. "Zaha Hadid Wins Pritzker," *Art in America*, May 2004, 45; Nicolai Ouroussoff, "First Woman Wins Pritzker," *Los Angeles Times*, March 22, 2004; Benjamin Forgey, "Hadid Is First Woman to Win Pritzker Prize," *Washington Post*, March 22, 2004; Robert W. Duffy, "Iraqi Native Is First Woman to Win Prestigious Prize for Architecture," *St. Louis Post-Dispatch*, March 22, 2004. For an analysis of the Pritzker jury citations and the gendered discourse of architectural genius, see Hilde Heynen, "Genius, Gender and Architecture: The Star System as Exemplified in the Pritzker Prize," *Women, Practice, Architecture*, special issue, *Architectural Theory Review* 17, nos. 2–3 (2012): 331–45.

2. Herbert Muschamp, "An Iraqi-Born Woman Wins Pritzker Architecture Award," *New York Times*, March 22, 2004; Herbert Muschamp, "Woman of Steel: Getting Her Architecture Built Was Zaha Hadid's Most Formidable Challenge," *New York Times*, March 28, 2004; Edwin Heathcote, "'Some Must Think I Deserve It,'" *Financial Times*, May 25, 2004; John Gallagher, "Designer Rejects Rational Order, Becomes First Woman to Win Pritzker Prize," *Knight Ridder Tribune Business News*, April 8, 2004; Nigel Coates, "Sometimes You Have to Behave Like a Diva if You Want to Get Stuff Built," *Independent*, May 30, 2004. For a criticism of this use of the term *diva*, see Robert Ivy, "Beyond Style," editorial, *Architectural Record*, May 1, 2004, 17. For an analysis of Zaha Hadid's more recent media image, see Igea Troiani, "Zaha: An Image of 'The Woman Architect,'" *Women, Practice, Architecture*, special issue, *Architectural Theory Review* 17, nos. 2–3 (2012): 346–64.

3. Stuart Jeffries, "Maybe They're Scared of Me: Zaha Hadid Was Once Famous for Not Getting Anything Built," *Guardian*, April 26, 2004.

4. Gallagher, "Designer Rejects Rational Order."

5. Muschamp, "Woman of Steel."

6. Ibid.

7. Ibid.

8. Ivy, "Beyond Style."

9. Carol Henderson, "Robert Venturi: No Architect Is an Island," letter to the editor, *New York Times*, May 19, 1991; Mike Capuzzo, "Plight of the Designing Woman," *Philadelphia Inquirer*, December 10, 1992; Jill Jordan Sieder, "A Building of Her Own," *U.S. News and World Report*, October 14, 1996, 67. On the collaborative nature of their firm, see Denise Scott Brown, "Room at the Top: Sexism and the Star System in Architecture," in *Architecture: A Place for Women*, ed. Ellen Perry Berkeley and Matilda McQuaid (Washington, DC: Smithsonian Institution Press, 1989), 239–40.

10. Bonnie Churchill, "Versatile Architect Wins Pritzker Prize," *Christian Science Monitor*, April 8, 1991; "Venturi Wins 1991 Pritzker Prize," *Architects' Journal*, April 17, 1991, 13.

11. Martin Filler, "Eyes on the Prize," *New Republic*, April 26 and May 3, 1999, 92.

12. James Sanders, "Robert Venturi: Denise Scott Brown: An Architectural Team to Reshape the American Landscape," *Los Angeles Times*, August 18, 1991. See also

Scott Brown, "Room at the Top," 241.

13. Scott Brown, "Room at the Top," 238, 242; Denise Scott Brown, "Sexism and the Star System in Architecture: A Lecture by Denise Scott Brown," synopsis published in *Proceedings of the West Coast Women's Design Conference, April 18–20, 1974, University of Oregon* (n.p.: West Coast Women's Design Conference, 1975), 20–21; "Architect Robert Venturi Is Named the 1991 Pritzker Architecture Prize Laureate," Pritzker Architecture Prize, http://www.pritzkerprize.com/1991/announcement, retrieved January 15, 2015.

14. "Architectural Partners in Japan Become the 2010 Pritzker Architecture Prize Laureates," Pritkzer Architecture Prize, http://www.pritzkerprize.com/2010/announcement, retrieved January 12, 2015.

15. Ann Lok Lui, "Working in the Shadows: Did the Pritzker Slight Wang Shu's Wife, Lu Wenyu?," *Architect's Newspaper*, April 25, 2012, http://www.archpaper.com/news/articles.asp?id=6016#.VLQazSvF-So, retrieved January 12, 2015.

16. Richard Waite, "Video Exclusive: Denise Scott Brown on Why She Deserves Pritzker Recognition," *Architects' Journal*, April 10, 2013, http://www.architectsjournal.co.uk/video-exclusive-denise-scott-brown-on-why-she-deserves-pritzker-recognition/8645333.article, retrieved January 14, 2015; Richard Waite, "Call for Denise Scott Brown to Be Given Pritzker Recognition," *Architects' Journal*, March 21, 2013; Rory Olcayto, "Pritzker Prize: Denise Scott Brown Should Have Won in '91," *Architects' Journal*, March 19, 2013.

17. "The Pritzker Architecture Prize Committee: Recognize Denise Scott Brown for Her Work in Robert Venturi's 1991 Prize," Change.org petition, https://www.change.org/p/the-pritzker-architecture-prize-committee-recognize-denise-scott-brown-for-her-work-in-robert-venturi-s-1991-prize, retrieved January 14, 2015; Alexandra Lange, "Architecture's Lean In Moment," *Metropolis Magazine*, July–August 2013, 59.

18. Robin Pogrebin, "Partner without the Prize," *New York Times*, April 17, 2013; Catriona Davies, "Denise Scott Brown: Architecture Favors 'Lone Male Genius' over Women," *CNN International*, May 29, 2013, http://edition.cnn.com/2013/05/01/business/denise-scott-brown-pritzker-prize, retrieved January 20, 2015.

19. Olcayto, "Pritzker Prize."

20. Colonel Pancake, wmh, salvatore, Standpipe, and Frank, comments made on "Denise Scott Brown Demands Pritzker Recognition," *Dezeen Magazine*, March 27, 2013, http://www.dezeen.com/2013/03/27/denise-scott-brown-demands-pritzker-recognition/, retrieved January 16, 2015.

21. Carolina A. Miranda, "Pritzker Architecture Prize Committee Denies Honors for Denise Scott Brown," *Architect*, June 14, 2013, http://www.architectmagazine.com/design/pritzker-architecture-prize-committee-refuses-to-honor-denise-scott-brown.aspx, retrieved January 20, 2015.

22. "Harvard Students Fire Back at Pritzker Jury's Response to Denise Scott Brown Petition," *Architectural Record*, July 11, 2013, http://archrecord.construction.com/news/2013/07/130711-harvard-design-denise-scott-brown-petition-pritzker-jury.asp, retrieved January 15, 2015.

23. Guy Horton, "Pritzker Prize Rejects Denise Scott Brown," *Huffington Post*, June 17, 2013, http://www.huffingtonpost.com/guy-horton/pritzker-prize-rejects-de_b_3445457.html, retrieved January 15, 2015.

24. Anna Kats, "The Architecture Community Responds to Pritzker's Denise Scott Brown Verdict," *Blouin ArtInfo*, June 18, 2013, http://blogs.artinfo.com/objectlessons/2013/06/18/the-architecture-community-responds-to-pritzkers-denise-scott-brown-verdict, retrieved January 15, 2015.

25. Ibid.

26. Beverly Willis, "The Lone Heroic Architect Is Passé," opinion pages, *New York Times*, July 15, 2014, http://www.nytimes.com/roomfordebate/2013/05/14/married

-to-an-award-winner/the-lone-heroic-architect-is-passe, retrieved January 20, 2015; Wendy Moonan, "AIA Awards 2014 Gold Medal to Julia Morgan," *Architectural Record*, December 16, 2013, http://archrecord.construction.com/news/2013/12/131216-aia -awards-2014-gold-medal-to-julia-morgan.asp, retrieved January 17, 2015; Lange, "Architecture's Lean In Moment," 78.

27. Cathleen McGuigan and Laura Raskin, "AIA 2013: National AIA Votes to Allow Two Individuals to Win Gold Medal," *Architectural Record*, June 4, 2013, http://archrecord .construction.com/news/2013/06/130604-new-york-aia-chapter-recommends-a -change-to-gold-medal-rules.asp, retrieved January 20, 2015.

28. Mark Alden Branch, "The Medal-Go-Round," *Progressive Architecture*, October 1994, 69; Kats, "The Architecture Community Responds to Pritzker's Denise Scott Brown Verdict."

29. Lange, "Architecture's Lean In Moment," 81.

30. "List of Architecture Prizes," Wikipedia.org, https://en.wikipedia.org/wiki/List_of _architecture_prizes, retrieved January 17, 2015; Willis, "The Lone Heroic Architect Is Passé."

31. Lange, "Architecture's Lean In Moment," 59.

32. Branch, "The Medal-Go-Round," 65–66.

33. Alex Frangos, "A Year after Pritzker, Doors Are Open for Architect," *Wall Street Journal*, March 23, 2005.

34. Moonan, "AIA Awards 2014 Gold Medal to Julia Morgan."

35. Bill Lacy, quoted by Branch, "The Medal-Go-Round," 108.

36. Branch, "The Medal-Go-Round," 66, 108.

37. Ned Cramer, "The Shigeru Ban Win Is a Big Deal," *Architect*, May 1, 2014, http:// www.architectmagazine.com/architects/the-shigeru-ban-win-is-a-big-deal_o .aspx, retrieved January 20, 2015; Robin Pogrebin, "Pritzker Architecture Prize Goes to Shigeru Ban," *New York Times*, March 24, 2014.

38. Kate Mosse, "History," Baileys Women's Prize for Fiction, http://www.womens prizeforfiction.co.uk/about/history, retrieved January 20, 2015.

39. "Architectural Record Announces Winners of First Annual Women in Architecture Awards," *Architectural Record*, August 12, 2014, http://archrecord.construction.com/news /2014/08/140812-architectural-record-winners-first-annual-women-in-architecture -awards.asp, retrieved January 20, 2015; Berkeley-Rupp Architecture Professorship and Prize, http://rupp.ced.berkeley.edu/prize, retrieved January 20, 2015, Beverly Willis Architecture Foundation, "BWAF Rolls Out Leadership Awards," June 30, 2014, http:// bwaf.org/bwaf-rolls-out-leadership-awards, retrieved January 20, 2015; Laura Mark, "AJ Women in Architecture Awards," *Architects' Journal*, November 25, 2014, http:// www.architectsjournal.co.uk/news/aj-women-in-architecture-awards-deadline -extended/8671996.article, retrieved April 6, 2015; Italcementi Group, "arcVision Prize—Women and Architecture," February 8, 2013, http://www.italcementigroup.com /ENG/Media+and+Communication/News/Building+and+Architecture/20130208.htm, retrieved January 20, 2015; Karissa Rosenfield, "Shereen Sherzad Wins the 2014 Tamayouz Women in Architecture and Construction Award," *ArchDaily*, November 4, 2014, http://www.archdaily.com/?p=563900, retrieved January 20, 2015.

40. "The Prize," Berkeley-Rupp Architecture Professorship and Prize, http://rupp.ced .berkeley.edu/prize.

41. Karen Burns, "Who Wants to Be a Woman Architect?," *Archiparlour*, May 2, 2012, http://archiparlour.org/who-wants-to-be-a-woman-architect, retrieved January 20, 2015.

42. Richard Waite, "'Women Need to Support Each Other,' Says Zaha after Winning Jane Drew Prize," *Architects' Journal*, April 20, 2012, http://www.architectsjournal .co.uk/news/daily-news/women-need-to-support-each-other-says-zaha-after -winning-jane-drew-prize/8629310.article, retrieved January 20, 2015.

43. Becky Anderson, "At Last, It's Zaha Hadid's Time to Shine," *CNN International*,

August 8, 2012, http://edition.cnn.com/2012/08/01/business/leading-women-zaha -hadid, retrieved January 20, 2015.

Chapter 5: Unforgetting Women Architects: A Confrontation with History and Wikipedia

1. On Hatshepsut, see Kara Cooney, *The Woman Who Would Be King: Hatshepsut's Rise to Power in Ancient Egypt* (New York: Crown, 2014), and Catharine H. Roehrig, Renée Dreyfus and Cathleen A. Keller, eds., *Hatshepsut, From Queen to Pharaoh* (New York: Metropolitan Museum of Art, and New Haven, CT: Yale University Press, 2005). This chapter draws on and expands an earlier article: Despina Stratigakos, "Unforget- ting Women Architects: From Pritzker to Wikipedia," *Places Journal*, June 2013, http:// places.designobserver.com/feature/unforgetting-women-architects-from-pritzker -to-wikipedia/37912, retrieved May 25, 2015.

2. International Archive of Women in Architecture, http://spec.lib.vt.edu/IAWA, retrieved May 25, 2015.

3. Christine Battersby, *Gender and Genius: Toward a Feminist Aesthetics* (London: Women's Press, 1989).

4. Natalie Kampen and Elizabeth G. Grossman, "Feminism and Methodology: Dynamics of Change in the History of Art and Architecture" (Working Paper no. 1212, Center for Research on Women, Wellesley College, Wellesley, MA, 1983), 9 ff; Cheryl Buckley, "Made in Patriarchy: Towards a Feminist Analysis of Women and Design," *Design Issues* 3 (Autumn 1986): 10–12; Abigail A. Van Slyck, "Women in Architecture and the Problems of Biogra- phy," *Gender and Design*, special issue, *Design Book Review* 25 (Summer 1992): 19–22.

5. Amanda Baillieu, "Architecture Is the Loser if We Censor History: Monographs Contribute to the Marginalisation of the Profession," *BDonline*, January 30, 2015, http://www.bdonline.co.uk/comment/architecture-is-the-loser-if-we-censor -history/5073506.article, retrieved January 30, 2015.

6. Helen Searing et al., "Equal and Unequal Partners, 1881–1970," in *Equal Partners: Men and Women Principals in Contemporary Architectural Practice* (Northampton, MA: Smith College Museum of Art, 1998), 22–39.

7. Denise Scott Brown, "Room at the Top: Sexism and the Star System in Architecture," in *Architecture: A Place for Women*, ed. Ellen Perry Berkeley and Matilda McQuaid (Washington, DC: Smithsonian Institution Press, 1989), 237–46.

8. Claire Potter, "Prikipedia? Or, Looking for the Women on Wikipedia," *Chronicle of Higher Education*, March 10, 2013, http://chronicle.com/blognetwork/tenuredradical, retrieved January 20, 2015.

9. Noam Cohen, "Define Gender Gap? Look Up Wikipedia's Contributor List," *New York Times*, January 30, 2011; Sue Gardner, "Nine Reasons Women Don't Edit Wikipedia (in Their Own Words)," *Sue Gardner's Blog*, February 19, 2011, http://suegardner.org /2011/02/19/nine-reasons-why-women-dont-edit-wikipedia-in-their-own-words, retrieved January 20, 2015.

10. Potter, "Prikipedia?"; Aviva Shen, "How Many Women Does It Take to Change Wikipedia?," *Smithsonian*, April 4, 2012, http://www.smithsonianmag.com/smithsonian -institution/how-many-women-does-it-take-to-change-wikipedia-171400755 /?no-ist=, retrieved January 20, 2015.

11. "Thekla Schild," *Wikipedia*, https://de.wikipedia.org/wiki/Thekla_Schild, retrieved January 20, 2015.

12. Despina Stratigakos, "'I Myself Want to Build:' Women, Architectural Education and the Integration of Germany's Technical Colleges," *Paedagogica Historica* 43, no. 6 (2007): 727–56.

13. Mia Ridge, "New Challenges in Digital History: Sharing Women's History on Wikipedia," paper delivered at the Women's History in the Digital World Conference, Bryn Mawr College, Bryn Mawr, PA, March 23, 2013, http://repository.brynmawr.edu /greenfield_conference/papers/saturday/37, retrieved January 20, 2015.

14. Dynamic National Archive Collection, Beverly Willis Architecture Foundation, http://www.bwaf.org/dna, retrieved May 25, 2015.

15. "List of Female Architects," *Wikipedia*, https://en.wikipedia.org/wiki/List_of _female_architects, retrieved January 21, 2015.

16. Amanda Filipacchi, "Wikipedia's Sexism Toward Female Novelists," *New York Times*, April 24, 2013.

17. Joyce Carol Oates, quoted by James Gleick, "Wikipedia's Women Problem," *New York Review of Books Blog*, April 29, 2013, http://www.nybooks.com/blogs/nyrblog /2013/apr/29/wikipedia-women-problem, retrieved January 21, 2015.

18. "List of Architects," *Wikipedia*, https://en.wikipedia.org/wiki/List_of_architects, retrieved January 21, 2015.

19. Gleick, "Wikipedia's Women Problem."

20. Filipacchi, "Wikipedia's Sexism Toward Female Novelists."

21. *East of Borneo*, "Unforgetting L.A. #2: MAK Center for Art and Architecture," event held December 14, 2013, http://www.eastofborneo.org/unforgetting2, retrieved January 21, 2015.

22. Storefront for Art and Architecture, "Wwwriting Series: Digital Invisibles," http:// www.storefrontnews.org/archive/2010?y=0&m=0&p=0&c=10&e=616, retrieved January 22, 2015. The edit-a-thon event was also part of a broader exhibition held at Storefront for Art and Architecture, *Letters to the Mayor*, which asked fifty architects (among them, two men) to write letters expressing concerns about the future of urban landscapes to political leaders worldwide.

23. Sue Gardner, comment made on November 24, 2010, on "Unlocking the Clubhouse: Five Ways to Encourage Women to Edit Wikipedia," *Sue Gardner's Blog*, November 14, 2010, http://suegardner.org/2010/11/14/unlocking-the-clubhouse -five-ways-to-encourage-women-to-edit-wikipedia/#comments, retrieved January 22, 2015.

Conclusion: Looking Back, Moving Forward

1. "Interview: Despina Stratigakos and Kelly Hayes McAlonie for Architect Barbie," *Mocoloco*, May 21, 2011, http://mocoloco.com/Interview-despina-stratigakos-and -kelly-hayes-mcalonie-for-architect-barbie, retrieved May 25, 2015, Lira Luis, "Architect Barbie Adventures: Meeting Mr. Wright," *Atelier Lira Luis Blog*, July 2011, http://liraluis.blogspot.com/2011/07/architect-barbie-adventures-meeting-mr .html, retrieved May 25, 2015; Megan Basnak, "Canvassing the Campus with Architect Barbie," *Archinect Blogs*, February 13, 2012, http://archinect.com/buffaloschool _stuudentlife/canvassing-the-campus-with-architect-barbie, retrieved May 25, 2015.

2. Stratigakos, "Unforgetting Women Architects"; *ArchiteXX*, "Women. Wikipedia. Design. #wikiD," event held on February 19, 2015, http://architexx.org/women -wikipedia-design-wikid, retrieved May 25, 2015.

3. Lori Brown, conversation with the author, March 19, 2015; "Down the Rabbit Hole: (Miss)Adventures in Wikipedia," *Tracings: A Newsletter of the Environmental Design Archives* 11, no. 1 (2015).

4. Patricia Arcilla, "#wikiD: Help ArchiteXX Add Women Architects to Wikipedia," *ArchDaily*, February 25, 2015, http://www.archdaily.com/?p=602663, retrieved March 31, 2015; "Grants: PEG/Parlour Inc/More Female Architects on Wikipedia," https:// meta.m.wikimedia.org/wiki/Grants:IEG/More_Female_Architects_on_Wikipedia #What_is_your_solution.3F, retrieved May 25, 2015.

5. Mark Lamster, "Why Are There Not Enough Women Architects?," *Dallas Morning News*, August 29, 2014, http://artsblog.dallasnews.com/2014/08/why-are-there-not -enough-women-architects.html, retrieved April 4, 2014 (refers to "Architect and Architectress," panel discussion held on August 25, 2014, at the Dallas Center for Architecture); Laura Mark, "Your Chance to Win a Ticket for Sold-Out AJ Women

in Architecture Luncheon," *Architects' Journal*, January 29, 2015, http://www
.architectsjournal.co.uk/news/your-chance-to-win-a-ticket-for-sold-out-aj-women
-in-architecture-luncheon/8677734.article, retrieved April 4, 2015 (refers to a
"Women in Architecture Luncheon" held on February 27, 2015, at Claridge's in London);
Los Angeles Chapter of the American Institute of Architects, "AIA/LA Announces
New Symposium on Women in Architecture: Powerful," http://aialosangeles.business
catalyst.com/article/powerful#.VSBYQE10z6g, retrieved April 4, 2015 (refers to
a "Powerful" symposium held on February 27, 2015, at the Annenberg Space for
Photography Skylight Studios in Los Angeles); "Women in Architecture," event held at
Manchester Metropolitan University Special Collections in Manchester, England, on
March 6, 2015, http://www.eventbrite.co.uk/e/women-in-architecture-tickets
-15400159291, retrieved April 4, 2015; "Women in Architecture Forum and Awards,"
event held at the McGraw-Hill Financial Headquarters in New York City, October 10,
2014, *Construction*, http://construction.com/events/2014/women-in-design, retrieved
April 4, 2015; "Equity by Design: Knowledge, Discussion, Action!," symposium held at
the San Francisco Art Institute on October 18, 2014, Missing 32% Project, http://the-
missing32percent.com/equity-by-design-10-18-14, retrieved April 4, 2015
6. Liam Otten, "Women in Architecture," Washington University in St. Louis Newsroom,
October 31, 2014, https://news.wustl.edu/news/Pages/27622.aspx, retrieved April 2, 2015.
7. AIA San Francisco and Equity by Design Committee, *Equity by Design: Knowledge,
Discussion, Action! 2014 Equity in Architecture Survey Report and Key Outcomes*,
report prepared by Annelise Pitts, Rosa Sheng, Eirik Evenhouse, and Ruohnan Hu (San
Francisco: AIA San Francisco, 2015), 23.
8. Rory Olcayto, "Discrimination Starts in the Studio," *Architects' Journal*, January 23,
2015, http://www.architectsjournal.co.uk/discrimination-starts-in-the-studio
/8676381.article, retrieved April 4, 2015; Patricia Arcilla, "AJ's 2015 Women in Architecture Survey Says 'Pay Gap' Is Slowly Closing," *ArchDaily*, January 23, 2015, http://
www.archdaily.com/?p=591058, retrieved April 2, 2015; Laura Mark, "Sexual Discrimination on the Rise—and Happening in Practices," *Architects' Journal*, January 23,
2015, http://www.architectsjournal.co.uk/events/wia/sexual-discrimination-on
-the-rise-and-happening-in-practices/8675344.article?blocktitle=Women-in
-Architecture-Survey-2015&contentID=12572, retrieved April 4, 2015; Laura Mark,
"Glass Ceiling Remains for Women in Architecture," *Architects' Journal*, January
23, 2015, http://www.architectsjournal.co.uk/home/events/wia/glass-ceiling
-remains-for-women-in-architecture/8675348.article, retrieved April 2, 2015. On
diversity and large corporate architecture firms, see also Kathryn H. Anthony,
Designing for Diversity: Gender, Race, and Ethnicity in the Architectural Profession
(Urbana: University of Illinois Press, 2001), 168–69.
9. Laura Mark, "Length of Training Huge Concern to Architecture Students," *Architects' Journal*, January 23, 2015, https://www.architectsjournal.co.uk/home/events
/wia/length-of-training-huge-concern-to-architecture-students/8675350.article,
retrieved April 2, 2015; Laura Mark, "Pay Inequity Starts on Entry to Profession,"
Architects' Journal, January 23, 2015, http://www.architectsjournal.co.uk/home
/events/wia/pay-inequality-starts-on-entry-to-profession/8675346.article, retrieved
April 4, 2015.

Bibliography

Adams, Annmarie, and Peta Tancred. *"Designing Women": Gender and the Architectural Profession*. Toronto: University of Toronto Press, 2000.

Agrest, Diana. *Architecture from Without: Theoretical Framings for a Critical Practice*. Cambridge, MA: MIT Press, 1993.

Agrest, Diana, Patricia Conway, and Leslie Kanes Weisman, eds. *The Sex of Architecture*. New York: Abrams, 1996.

Ahrentzen, Sherry. "The Space between the Studs: Feminism and Architecture." *Signs* 29, no. 1 (2003): 179–206.

Ahrentzen, Sherry, and Kathryn H. Anthony. "Sex, Stars, and Studios: A Look at Gendered Educational Practices in Architecture." *Journal of Architectural Education* 47, no. 1 (1993): 11–29.

Ahrentzen, Sherry, and Linda N. Groat. "Rethinking Architectural Education: Patriarchal Conventions and Alternative Visions from the Perspectives of Women Faculty." *Journal of Architectural and Planning Research* 9, no. 2 (1992): 1–17.

AIA San Francisco and Equity by Design Committee. *Equity by Design: Knowledge, Discussion, Action! 2014 Equity in Architecture Survey Report and Key Outcomes*. Report prepared by Annelise Pitts, Rosa Sheng, Eirik Evenhouse, and Ruohnan Hu. San Francisco: AIA San Francisco, 2015.

Aileen. "Wanted: Women Architects! To Do Away with Domestic Difficulties." *Irish Times*, February 18, 1939.

Alexander, Ella. "Architect Barbie." *Vogue* (U.K.), March 1, 2011. http://www.vogue .co.uk/news/2011/03/01/barbie-the-architect-launches.

Allaback, Sarah. *The First American Women Architects*. Urbana: University of Illinois Press, 2008.

American Architectural Foundation. *"That Exceptional One": Women in American Architecture, 1888–1988*. Washington, DC: American Architectural Foundation, 1988.

American Builder and Journal of Art. "Women in Art." September 1, 1872, 52.

American Institute of Architects. "Resolution 15–1, Equity in Architecture." *2015 AIA National Convention and Design Exposition: Official Delegate Information Booklet*. Washington, DC: American Institute of Architects, 2015, 15–16.

———. "Women in Architecture Toolkit." October 2013. http://issuu.com/aiadiv/docs /women_in_architecture_toolkit.

American Institute of Architects LinkedIn Forum. "Fetish in Pink." March–June 2011. http://www.linkedin.com/groupItem?view=&srchtype=discussedNews&gid =113822&item=45564786&type=member&trk=eml-anet_dig-b_pd-ttl-cn.

Anderson, Becky. "At Last, It's Zaha Hadid's Time to Shine." *CNN International*, August 8, 2012. http://edition.cnn.com/2012/08/01/business/leading-women-zaha-hadid.

Anderson, Lamar. "How Women Are Climbing Architecture's Career Ladder." *Curbed*, March 17, 2014. http://curbed.com/archives/2014/03/17/how-women-are-climbing -architectures-career-ladder.php.

Anthony, Kathryn H. *Designing for Diversity: Gender, Race, and Ethnicity in the*

Architectural Profession. Urbana: University of Illinois Press, 2001.

ArchDaily. "'Ladies (and Gents) Who Lunch with Architect Barbie' Event." October 13, 2011. http://www.archdaily.com/?p=175512.

Architects' Journal. Women in Practice. Special issue, *Architects' Journal*, January 12, 2012.

———. "Venturi Wins 1991 Pritzker Prize." April 17, 1991, 13.

Architectural Record. "Architectural Record Announces Winners of First Annual Women in Architecture Awards." August 12, 2014. http://archrecord.construction .com/news/2014/08/140812-architectural-record-winners-first-annual-women -in-architecture-awards.asp.

———. "Harvard Students Fire Back at Pritzker Jury's Response to Denise Scott Brown Petition." July 11, 2013. http://archrecord.construction.com/news/2013/07/130711 -harvard-design-denise-scott-brown-petition-pritzker-jury.asp.

ArchiteXX. "Women. Wikipedia. Design. #wikiD," February 19, 2015. http://architexx .org/women-wikipedia-design-wikid.

Arcilla, Patricia. "AJ's 2015 Women in Architecture Survey Says 'Pay Gap' Is Slowly Closing." *ArchDaily*, January 23, 2015.

———. "#wikiD: Help ArchiteXX Add Women Architects to Wikipedia." *ArchDaily*, February 25, 2015. http://www.archdaily.com/?p=602663.

Art in America. "Zaha Hadid Wins Pritzker." May 2004, 45.

Attfield, Judy, and Pat Kirkham, eds. *A View from the Interior: Women and Design*. London: Women's Press, 1989.

Baillieu, Amanda. "Architecture Is the Loser if We Censor History: Monographs Contribute to the Marginalisation of the Profession." *BDonline*, January 30, 2015. http://www.bdonline.co.uk/comment/architecture-is-the-loser-if-we-censor -history/5073506.article.

Baker, Paula. "The Domestication of Politics: Women and American Political Society, 1780–1920." *American Historical Review* 89, no. 3 (1984): 620–47.

Bartning, Otto. "Sollen Damen bauen?" [Should ladies build?] *Die Welt der Frau* (*Gartenlaube*), no. 40 (1911): 625–26.

Basnak, Megan. "Canvassing the Campus with Architect Barbie." *Archinect Blogs*, February 13, 2012. http://archinect.com/buffaloschool_stuudentlife/canvassing -the-campus-with-architect-barbie.

Battersby, Christine. *Gender and Genius: Toward a Feminist Aesthetics*. London: Women's Press, 1989.

Beck, Ernest. "Making the Mold: The Lack of Diversity in Architecture Isn't a Simple Problem, but There Are Better and Worse Ways to Approach the Issue." *Architect*, July 2, 2012. http://www.architectmagazine.com/practice/best-practices/making -progress-with-diversity-in-architecture_o.

Beem, Lulu Stoughton. "Women in Architecture: A Plea Dating from 1884." *Inland Architect* 15 (December 1971): 6.

Berkeley, Ellen Perry. "Women in Architecture." *Architectural Forum*, September 1972, 46–53.

Berkeley, Ellen Perry, and Matilda McQuaid, eds. *Architecture: A Place for Women*. Washington, DC: Smithsonian Institution Press, 1989.

Bethune, Louise. "Women and Architecture." *Inland Architect and News Record* 17, no. 2 (1891): 20–21.

Beverly Willis Architecture Foundation. "BWAF Rolls Out Leadership Awards." June 30, 2014. http://bwaf.org/bwaf-rolls-out-leadership-awards.

———. "Industry Leaders Roundtable Program." http://bwaf.org/roundtable /roundtable-about.

Birkby, Phyllis. "Herspace." *Making Room: Women and Architecture*. Special issue, *Heresies* 3, no. 3, issue 11 (1981): 28–29.

Bloomer, Jennifer, ed. *Architecture and the Feminine: Mop-Up Work*. Special issue, *Any*, January/February 1994.

Bonomo, Josephine. "Architecture Is Luring Women." *New York Times*, April 2, 1977.

Boquiren, Lisa. "In Equality—Architect Barbie's Journey to the Pritzker." *Metropolis*, July 9, 2013. http://www.metropolismag.com/Point-of-View/July-2013/In-equality -Architect-Barbies-Journey-to-the-Pritzker.

———. "What Can a Toy Do for Architecture?" *Metropolis*, November 2011. http:// www.metropolismag.com/Point-of-View/November-2011/What-can-a-toy-do-for -architecture.

Branch, Mark Alden. "The Medal-Go-Round." *Progressive Architecture*, October 1994, 65–69, 108.

Branton, Harriet. "The Forgotten Lady Architect." *Observer-Reporter* (Washington, PA), April 23, 1983.

British Architect. "Women as Architects." January 5, 1900, 16–17.

Brown, Lori, ed. *Feminist Practices: Interdisciplinary Approaches to Women in Architecture*. Farnham, Surrey, England: Ashgate, 2011.

Brown, Lori, and Nina Freedman. "Women in Architecture: Statistics for the Academy." *Indigogo*. https://www.indiegogo.com/projects/women-in-architecture.

Brown, Mabel. "Women in Profession: VII—Architecture." *San Francisco Chronicle*, September 24, 1905.

Buckley, Cheryl. "Made in Patriarchy: Towards a Feminist Analysis of Women and Design." *Design Issues* 3 (Autumn 1986): 3–14.

Building Age. "What a Woman Architect Could Do." January 1, 1911, 38.

Burns, Karen. "The Elephant in Our Parlour: Everyday Sexism in Architecture." *Archiparlour*, August 20, 2014. http://archiparlour.org/the-elephant-in-our-parlour -everyday-sexism-in-architecture.

———. "A Girl's Own Adventure: Gender in Contemporary Architectural Theory Anthology." *Journal of Architectural Education* 65, no. 2 (2012): 125–34.

———. "Who Wants to Be a Woman Architect?" *Archiparlour*, May 2, 2012. http:// archiparlour.org/who-wants-to-be-a-woman-architect.

Bustillo, Miguel. "Search Is On for Hot Stuff." *Wall Street Journal*, December 8, 2011.

Butcher, Luke. "Architect Barbie." *Luke Butcher Blog*, April 6, 2011. http://lukebutcher .blogspot.com/2011/04/architect-barbie.html.

Capuzzo, Mike. "Plight of the Designing Woman." *Philadelphia Inquirer*, December 10, 1992.

Chen, Stefanos. "In Architecture, a Glass Ceiling." *Wall Street Journal* online, August 21, 2014. http://www.wsj.com/articles/in-architecture-a-glass-ceiling-1408633998.

Chicago Daily Tribune. "Successful Woman Architect." August 26, 1896.

———. "These Girls Are Architects: Their Designs for a Hospital in San Francisco Have Been Accepted." December 15, 1894.

———. "U. S. Women Architects Number 379, Count Shows." May 21, 1939.

Christian Science Monitor. "Shakespeare Memorial Design Explained by Woman Architect." January 6, 1928.

———. "Women Architects." September 12, 1921.

Churchill, Bonnie. "Versatile Architect Wins Pritzker Prize." *Christian Science Monitor*, April 8, 1991.

Cincinnati Enquirer. "Women Architects." September 11, 1880.

Clark, Justine. "Six Myths about Women and Architecture." *Archiparlour*, September 6, 2014. http://archiparlour.org/six-myths-about-women-and-architecture.

Clausen, Meredith L. "The Ecole des Beaux-Arts: Toward a Gendered History." *Journal of the Society of Architecture Historians* 69, no. 2 (2010): 153–61.

Click. Directed by Frank Coraci. Culver City, CA: Columbia Pictures Corporation, 2006. DVD.

Coates, Nigel. "Sometimes You Have to Behave Like a Diva if You Want to Get Stuff Built." *Independent*, May 30, 2004.

Cohen, Jodi S. "Ground Zero of Affirmative Action Issue: As Michigan Voters Decide Whether Gender, Race Should Be Factors in Jobs and Admissions, the Outcome Could Affect the National Debate." *Chicago Tribune*, October 19, 2006.

Cohen, Noam. "Define Gender Gap? Look Up Wikipedia's Contributor List." *New York Times*, January 30, 2011.

Cohen, Philip. "More Women Are Doctors and Lawyers than Ever—but Progress Is Stalling." *Atlantic*, December 11, 2012. http://www.theatlantic.com/sexes /archive/2012/12/more-women-are-doctors-and-lawyers-than-ever-but-progress -is-stalling/266115.

Coleman, Debra, Elizabeth Danze, and Carol Henderson, eds. *Architecture and Feminism*. New York: Princeton Architectural Press, 1996.

Colomina, Beatriz, ed. *Sexuality and Space*. New York: Princeton Architectural Press, 1992.

Cooney, Kara. *The Woman Who Would Be King: Hatshepsut's Rise to Power in Ancient Egypt*. New York: Crown, 2014.

Countryside. "Women Architects." *Arthur's Home Magazine* 53 (June 1885): 368.

Cramer, Ned. "The Shigeru Ban Win Is a Big Deal." *Architect*, May 1, 2014. http://www .architectmagazine.com/architects/the-shigeru-ban-win-is-a-big-deal_o.aspx.

Daily Boston Globe. "Gropius Tells Lacks of Properly Built Homes." May 22, 1938.

Danze, Elizabeth, and Carol Henderson, eds. *Architecture and Feminism*. New York: Princeton Architectural Press, 1996.

Darley, Gillian. "A Stage of Her Own." *Guardian*, January 29, 2011.

Daussig, Fritz. "Ein weiblicher Architekt" [A female architect]. *Daheim* 45, no. 48 (1909): 11–14.

Davies, Catriona. "Denise Scott Brown: Architecture Favors 'Lone Male Genius' over Women." *CNN International*, May 29, 2013. http://edition.cnn.com/2013/05/01 /business/denise-scott-brown-pritzker-prize.

[Davison, Thomas Raggles]. "May Women Practise Architecture?" *British Architect*, February 21, 1902.

De Graft-Johnson, Ann, Sandra Manley, and Clara Greed. *Why Do Women Leave Architecture?* Bristol: University of the West of England–Bristol, and London: Royal Institute of British Architects, 2003.

Derringer, Jaime. "Top 10 of 2011: Design." *USA Character Approved Blog*, December 7, 2011. http://www.characterblog.com/design/top-10-of-2011-design.

Dezeen Magazine. "Denise Scott Brown Demands Pritzker Recognition." March 27, 2013. http://www.dezeen.com/2013/03/27/denise-scott-brown-demands-pritzker -recognition.

Doumato, Lamia. *Women as Architects: A Historical View*. Monticello, IL: Vance Bibliographies, 1978.

Duffy, Robert W. "Iraqi Native Is First Woman to Win Prestigious Prize for Architecture." *St. Louis Post-Dispatch*, March 22, 2004.

Duncan, Jane. "Why Are So Many Women Leaving Architecture?" *Guardian*, August 7, 2013. http://www.theguardian.com/women-in-leadership/2013/aug/07/women -leaving-architecture-profession.

Durning, Louise, and Richard Wrigley. *Gender and Architecture*. Chichester, England: Wiley, 2000.

East of Borneo. "Unforgetting L.A. #2: MAK Center for Art and Architecture." http:// www.eastofborneo.org/unforgetting2.

Edelman, Judith. "Task Force on Women: The AIA Responds to a Growing Presence." In *Architecture: A Place for Women*, ed. Ellen Perry Berkeley and Matilda McQuaid, 117–23. Washington, DC: Smithsonian Institution Press, 1989.

Elle Decor. "What We Love." July–August 2011, 30.

Ennis, Thomas W. "Women Gain Role in Architecture: Profession Yields Slowly." *New York Times*, March 13, 1960.

Erskine, Lucile. "Woman in Architecture." *Cincinnati Enquirer*, October 8, 1911.

Esperdy, Gabrielle. "The Incredible True Adventures of the Architectress in America." *Places Journal*, September 2012. http://placesjournal.org/article/the-incredible -true-adventures-of-the-architectress-in-america.

Fenten, D. X. *Ms. Architect.* Philadelphia: Westminster, 1977.

Filipacchi, Amanda. "Wikipedia's Sexism toward Female Novelists." *New York Times*, April 24, 2013.

Filler, Martin. "Eyes on the Prize." *New Republic*, April 26 and May 3, 1999, 86–94.

Finch, Lauren. "Dreaming of the Future: AIA Chicago Joins CPS [Chicago Public Schools] for Inaugural Barbie Architect Workshop." *Chicago Architect*, January/ February 2013. http://mydigimag.rrd.com/article/Dreaming_of_the_Future /1275362/140831/article.html.

Forgey, Benjamin. "Hadid Is First Woman to Win Pritzker Prize." *Washington Post*, March 22, 2004.

Fowler, Bridget, and Fiona Wilson. "Women Architects and Their Discontents." *Sociology* 38, no. 1 (2004): 101–19.

Frangos, Alex. "A Year after Pritzker, Doors Are Open for Architect." *Wall Street Journal*, March 23, 2005.

Fraser, Graham. "Architecture Students Abused, Report Says: Teaching Environment at Carleton School Called Discriminatory, Unprofessional, Sexist." *Globe and Mail*, December 23, 1992.

Friedman, Alice. "A Feminist Practice in Architectural History?" *Gender and Design*. Special issue, *Design Book Review* 25 (Summer 1992): 16–18.

———. *Women and the Making of the Modern House: A Social and Architectural History*. New Haven, CT: Yale University Press, 2007.

Frost, Henry Atherton, and William Richard Sears. *Women in Architecture and Landscape Architecture*. Northampton, MA: Smith College, 1928.

Futterman, Ellen. "Women in Architecture: 100 Years and Counting." *St. Louis Post-Dispatch*, May 7, 1989.

Gallagher, John. "Designer Rejects Rational Order, Becomes First Woman to Win Pritzker Prize." *Knight Ridder Tribune Business News*, April 8, 2004.

Gardner, Sue. "Nine Reasons Women Don't Edit Wikipedia (in Their Own Words)." *Sue Gardner's Blog*, February 19, 2011. http://suegardner.org/2011/02/19/nine-reasons -why-women-dont-edit-wikipedia-in-their-own-words.

———. "Unlocking the Clubhouse: Five Ways to Encourage Women to Edit Wikipedia." *Sue Gardner's Blog*, November 14, 2010. http://suegardner.org/2010/11/14 /unlocking-the-clubhouse-five-ways-to-encourage-women-to-edit-wikipedia /#comments.

Garfinkle, Charlene G. "Women at Work: The Design and Decoration of the Woman's Building at the 1893 World's Columbian Exposition." Ph.D. diss., University of California, Santa Barbara, 1996.

Genevro, Rosalie, and Anne Rieselbach. "A Conversation with Susana Torre." Architectural League of New York Web Feature, *Women in American Architecture: 1977 and Today*. http://archleague.org/2013/09/susana-torre.

Genz, Stéphanie, and Benjamin A. Brabon. *Postfeminism: Cultural Texts and Theories*. Edinburgh, Scotland: Edinburgh University Press, 2009.

Ghirardo, Diane. "Cherchez la femme: Where Are the Women in Architectural Studies?" In *Desiring Practices: Architecture, Gender and the Interdisciplinary*, ed. Katerina Rüedi, Sarah Wigglesworth, and Duncan McCorquodale, 156–73. London: Black Dog, 1996.

Gius, Barbara. "Women Virtually Absent in Field of Architecture." *Los Angeles Times*, March 16, 1975.

Glancey, Jonathan. "The Best Architecture of 2011: Jonathan Glancey's Choice." *Guardian*, December 5, 2011.

Gleick, James. "Wikipedia's Women Problem." *New York Review of Books Blog*, April 29, 2013. http://www.nybooks.com/blogs/nyrblog/2013/apr/29/wikipedia-women -problem.

Globe and Mail. "Women Architects Needed." April 24, 1962.

Goldberger, Paul. "Women Architects Building Influence in a Profession That Is 98.8% Male. *New York Times*, May 18, 1974.

Greed, Clara H. *Women and Planning: Creating Gendered Realities*. London: Routledge, 1994.

Griffiths, Diana. "A Lost Legacy." *Archiparlour*, April 18, 2012. http://archiparlour.org /authors/diana-griffiths.

Groat, Linda N., and Sherry B. Ahrentzen. "Voices for Change in Architectural Education: Seven Facets of Transformation from the Perspectives of Faculty Women." *Journal of Architectural Education* 50, no. 4 (1997): 271–85.

Guerrilla Girls. *The Guerrilla Girls' Bedside Companion to the History of Western Art*. New York: Penguin, 1998.

Harris, Melissa. "Mattel Launching Computer Engineer Barbie: Society of Women Engineers CEO Helps Design New Career Doll." *Chicago Tribune*, April 14, 2010.

Hartmann, Margaret. "New Architect Barbie Designs Her Own Dream House." *Jezebel*, February 22, 2011. http://jezebel.com/5766877/new-architect-barbie-designs-her -own-dream-house.

Hayden, Dolores. *The Grand Domestic Revolution: A History of Feminist Designs for American Homes, Neighborhoods, and Cities*. Cambridge, MA: MIT Press, 1981.

Heathcote, Edwin. "'Some Must Think I Deserve It.'" *Financial Times*, May 25, 2004.

Henderson, Carol. "Robert Venturi: No Architect Is An Island." Letter to the editor, *New York Times*, May 19, 1991.

Hewitt, Karen. "Does Architect Barbie Play with Blocks?" *Learning Materials Workshop Blog*, February 22, 2011. http://learningmaterialswork.com/blog/2011/02/does -architect-barbie-play-with-blocks.

Heynen, Hilde. "Genius, Gender and Architecture: The Star System as Exemplified in the Pritzker Prize." *Women, Practice, Architecture*. Special issue, *Architectural Theory Review* 17, nos. 2–3 (2012): 331–45.

Heynen, Hilde, and Gülsüm Baydar, eds. *Negotiating Domesticity: Spatial Productions of Gender in Modern Architecture*. London: Routledge, 2005.

Hicks, Margaret. "The Tenement-House Problem—II." *American Architect and Building News*, July 31, 1880.

Holan, Jerri. "Architect Barbie: Role Model or Ridiculous?" *UrbDeZine San Francisco*, November 30, 2011. http://sanfrancisco.urbdezine.com/2011/11/30/architect -barbie-role-model-or-ridiculous.

Horton, Guy. "Pritzker Prize Rejects Denise Scott Brown." *Huffington Post*, June 17, 2013. http://www.huffingtonpost.com/guy-horton/pritzker-prize-rejects-de_b _3445457.html.

Horton, Inge Schaefer. *Early Women Architects of the San Francisco Bay Area: The Lives and Work of Fifty Professionals, 1890–1951*. Jefferson, NC: McFarland, 2010.

Hughes, Francesca, ed. *The Architect: Reconstructing Her Practice*. Cambridge, MA: MIT Press, 1998.

Huxtable, Ada Louise. "The Last Profession to Be 'Liberated' by Women." *New York Times*, March 13, 1977.

indesignlive. "Architect Barbie." February 24, 2011. http://www.indesignlive.com /articles/in-review/architect-barbie.

Innis, Sherrie A. "Barbie Gets a Bum Rap: Barbie's Place in the World of Dolls." In *The Barbie Chronicles: A Living Doll Turns Forty*, ed. Yona Zeldis McDonough, 177–81. New York: Touchstone, 1999.

Irish Times. "A Little Imagination Could Improve Look of 'Suburbia.'" June 2, 1972.

Italcementi Group. "arcVision Prize—Women and Architecture." February 8, 2013. http://www.italcementigroup.com/ENG/Media+and+Communication/News /Building+and+Architecture/20130208.htm.

Ivy, Robert. "Beyond Style." Editorial, *Architectural Record*, May 1, 2004, 17.

Jeffries, Stuart. "Maybe They're Scared of Me: Zaha Hadid Was Once Famous for Not Getting Anything Built." *Guardian*, April 26, 2004.

Johnson, Carolyn R. *Women in Architecture: An Annotated Bibliography and Guide to Sources of Information*. Monticello, IL: Council of Planning Librarians, 1974.

Journal of the Society of Architects. "Architecture as a Profession for Women." Vol. 5, no. 53 (1912): 188–89.

———. "Why Not Women Architects? Great Demand and No Supply." Vol. 6, no. 70 (1913): 393–94.

Kaji-O'Grady, Sandra. "Does Motherhood + Architecture = No Career?" *ArchitectureAU*, November 20, 2014. http://architectureau.com/articles/does-motherhood -architecture-no-career.

Kampen, Natalie, and Elizabeth G. Grossman. "Feminism and Methodology: Dynamics of Change in the History of Art and Architecture." Working Paper no. 1212, Center for Research on Women, Wellesley College, Wellesley, MA, 1983.

Kats, Anna. "The Architecture Community Responds to Pritzker's Denise Scott Brown Verdict." *Blouin ArtInfo*, June 18, 2013. http://blogs.artinfo.com/objectlessons /2013/06/18/the-architecture-community-responds-to-pritzkers-denise-scott -brown-verdict.

Kay, Jane Holtz. "Women Architects—A Liberated Elite?" *Boston Globe*, September 13, 1970.

Kennedy, Margrit. "Seven Hypotheses on Female and Male Principles in Architecture." *Making Room: Women and Architecture*. Special issue, *Heresies* 3, no. 3, issue 11 (1981): 12–13.

Kingsly, Karen. "Rethinking Architectural History from a Gender Perspective." In *Voices in Architectural Education: Cultural Politics and Pedagogy*, ed. Thomas A. Dutton, 249–64. New York: Bergin and Garvey, 1991.

Kirkham, Pat, ed. *Women Designers in the USA: 1900–2000*. New Haven, CT: Yale University Press, 2000.

Kostof, Spiro, ed. *The Architect: Chapters in the History of the Profession*. New York: Oxford University Press, 1977.

Lamster, Mark. "Why Are There Not Enough Women Architects?" *Dallas Morning News*, August 29, 2014. http://artsblog.dallasnews.com/2014/08/why-are-there-not -enough-women-architects.html.

Lane, Jessica. "The Audacity of Architect Barbie." *EHDD*, March 3, 2011. http://www .ehdd.com/4440.

Lange, Alexandra. "Architecture's Lean In Moment." *Metropolis Magazine*, July–August 2013, 58–59, 78–81.

———. "Girl Talk." *Dwell*, July–August 2012, 92–94.

Levinson, Nancy. "Architect Barbie." *Design Observer*, February 18, 2011. http:// designobserver.com/feature/architect-barbie/24718.

Lipowicz, Alice. "Architects Make Gains, but Few Elevated to Top." *Crain's New York Business* 17, no. 25 (2001): 32.

Lobell, Mimi. "The Buried Treasure: Women's Ancient Architectural Heritage." In *Architecture: A Place for Women*, ed. Ellen Perry Berkeley and Matilda McQuaid, 139–57. Washington, DC: Smithsonian Institution Press, 1989.

Loper, Mary Lou. "Wanted: More Women Architects." *Los Angeles Times*, November 11, 1960.

Lui, Ann Lok. "Working in the Shadows: Did the Pritzker Slight Wang Shu's Wife, Lu Wenyu?" *Architect's Newspaper*, April 25, 2012. http://www.archpaper.com/news/articles.asp?id=6016#.VLQazSvF-So.

Luis, Lira. "Architect Barbie Adventures: Meeting Mr. Wright." *Atelier Lira Luis Blog*, July 2011. http://liraluis.blogspot.com/2011/07/architect-barbie-adventures-meeting-mr.html.

Maasberg, Ute, and Regina Prinz. *Die Neuen kommen! Weibliche Avantgarde in der Architektur der zwanziger Jahre* [Here come the new ones! Female avantgardists in 1920s architecture]. Hamburg: Junius, 2004.

Making Room: Women and Architecture. Special issue, *Heresies* 3, no. 3, issue 11 (1981).

Manchester Guardian. "Woman Architect's Prize: Winning Design for New Shakespeare Memorial Theater." January 6, 1928.

Mark, Laura. "AJ Women in Architecture Awards." *Architects' Journal*, November 25, 2014. http://www.architectsjournal.co.uk/news/aj-women-in-architecture-awards-deadline-extended/8671996.article.

——— . "Bullying on the Rise in Architecture School." *Architects' Journal*, January 10, 2014. https://www.architectsjournal.co.uk/home/events/wia/bullying-on-the-rise-in-architecture-school/8657351.article.

——— . "88% Women Say Having Children Puts Them at a Disadvantage." *Architects' Journal*, January 10, 2014. https://www.architectsjournal.co.uk/home/events/wia/88-women-say-having-children-puts-them-at-disadvantage/8657348.article.

——— . "Gender Pay Gap: 'Beyond Shocking.'" *Architects' Journal*, May 2, 2014. http://www.architectsjournal.co.uk/news/gender-pay-gap-beyond-shocking/8662077.article.

——— . "Gender Pay Gap Worst in America." *Architects' Journal*, January 10, 2014. http://www.architectsjournal.co.uk/home/events/wia/gender-pay-gap-worst-in-america/8657355.article.

——— . "Glass Ceiling Remains for Women in Architecture." *Architects' Journal*, January 23, 2015. http://www.architectsjournal.co.uk/home/events/wia/glass-ceiling-remains-for-women-in-architecture/8675348.article.

——— . "Length of Training Huge Concern to Architecture Students." *Architects' Journal*, January 23, 2015. https://www.architectsjournal.co.uk/home/events/wia/length-of-training-huge-concern-to-architecture-students/8675350.article.

——— . "Pay Gap Widens: Women Architects Earn Less than Men." *Architects' Journal*, January 10, 2014. https://www.architectsjournal.co.uk/home/events/wia/pay-gap-widens-women-architects-earn-less-than-men/8657346.article.

——— . "Pay Inequity Starts on Entry to Profession." *Architects' Journal*, January 23, 2015. http://www.architectsjournal.co.uk/home/events/wia/pay-inequality-starts-on-entry-to-profession/8675346.article.

——— . "Sexual Discrimination on the Rise—and Happening in Practices." *Architects' Journal*, January 23, 2015. http://www.architectsjournal.co.uk/events/wia/sexual-discrimination-on-the-rise-and-happening-in-practices/8675344.article?blocktitle=Women-in-Architecture-Survey-2015&contentID=12572.

——— . "Sexual Discrimination on the Rise for Women in Architecture." *Architects' Journal*, January 10, 2014. https://www.architectsjournal.co.uk/home/events/wia/sexual-discrimination-on-the-rise-for-women-in-architecture/8657345.article.

——— . "Survey Shows Shocking Lack of Respect for Women Architects." *Architects' Journal*, January 10, 2014. https://www.architectsjournal.co.uk/survey-shows-shocking-lack-of-respect-for-women-architects/8657343.article.

——— . "Your Chance to Win a Ticket for Sold-Out AJ Women in Architecture Luncheon." *Architects' Journal*, January 29, 2015. http://www.architectsjournal

.co.uk/news/your-chance-to-win-a-ticket-for-sold-out-aj-women-in-architecture
-luncheon/8677734.article.

Marshall, Mary. "The Call of Architecture for Women Workers: Women Have to Be Housekeepers—Why Should Men Plan the House?" *New York Tribune*, August 3, 1912.

Martin, Brenda, and Penny Sparke, eds. *Women's Places: Architecture and Design, 1860–1960*. Abingdon, Oxon, England: Routledge, 2003.

Matthewson, Gill. "'Nothing Else Will Do': The Call for Gender Equality in Architecture in Britain." *Women, Practice, Architecture*. Special issue, *Architectural Theory Review* 17, nos. 2–3 (2012): 245–59.

Matrix. *Making Space: Women and the Man Made Environment*. London: Pluto, 1984.

McDonough, Yona Zeldis, ed. *The Barbie Chronicles: A Living Doll Turns Forty*. New York: Touchstone, 1999.

McGuigan, Cathleen, and Laura Raskin. "AIA 2013: National AIA Votes to Allow Two Individuals to Win Gold Medal." *Architectural Record*, June 4, 2013. http://archrecord.construction.com/news/2013/06/130604-new-york-aia-chapter-recommends-a-change-to-gold-medal-rules.asp.

McLeod, Mary, "Reflections on Feminism and Modern Architecture." *Harvard Design Magazine*, Spring/Summer 2004, 64–67.

McQuaid, Matilda, and Magdalene Droste. *Lilly Reich: Designer and Architect*. New York: Museum of Modern Art, 1996.

Meisels, Sophia Saravamartha. "Half of Greek Architects Are Women." *Jerusalem Post*, December 24, 1967.

Minter, Harriet. "Sexism in Architecture: On the Rise." *Guardian*, January 13, 2014. http://www.theguardian.com/women-in-leadership/2014/jan/13/women-in-architecture-sexism.

Miranda, Carolina A. "Pritzker Architecture Prize Committee Denies Honors for Denise Scott Brown." *Architect*, June 14, 2013. http://www.architectmagazine.com/design/pritzker-architecture-prize-committee-refuses-to-honor-denise-scott-brown.aspx.

Mitchell, Josh. "Women Notch Progress: Females Now Constitute One-Third of Nation's Ranks of Doctors and Lawyers." *Wall Street Journal*, December 4, 2012.

Mizra and Nacey Research. *The Architectural Profession in Europe, 2014: A Sector Study Commissioned by the Architects' Council of Europe*. Brussels: Architects' Council of Europe, 2015. http://www.ace-cae.eu/fileadmin/New_Upload/7._Publications/Sector_Study/2014/EN/2014_CN_FULL.pdf.

Mocoloco. "Interview: Despina Stratigakos and Kelly Hayes McAlonie for Architect Barbie." May 21, 2011. http://mocoloco.com/interview-despina-stratigakos-and-kelly-hayes-mcalonie-for-architect-barbie.

Modern Review. "Where Are the Women Architects?" September 1923, 355.

Moonan, Wendy. "AIA Awards 2014 Gold Medal to Julia Morgan." *Architectural Record*, December 16, 2013. http://archrecord.construction.com/news/2013/12/131216-aia-awards-2014-gold-medal-to-julia-morgan.asp.

Morris, Yvette. "Q&A with Tamarah Begay, AIA: Navajo Nation Architect, Barbie Ambassador." *AIArchitect*, August 23, 2013. http://www.aia.org/practicing/AIAB099854.

Mosse, Kate. "History." Baileys Women's Prize for Fiction. http://www.womensprizeforfiction.co.uk/about/history.

Muschamp, Herbert. "An Iraqi-Born Woman Wins Pritzker Architecture Award." *New York Times*, March 22, 2004.

———. "Woman of Steel: Getting Her Architecture Built Was Zaha Hadid's Most Formidable Challenge." *New York Times*, March 28, 2004.

National Architectural Accrediting Board. *2014 Annual Report from the National Architectural Accrediting Board, Inc., Part I: Programs, Students, and Degrees*.

Washington, DC: National Architectural Accrediting Board, 2015.

———. *2014 Annual Report from the National Architectural Accrediting Board, Inc., Part III: Faculty*. Washington, DC: National Architectural Accrediting Board, 2015.

National Council of Architectural Registration Boards. *2014 NCARB by the Numbers*. Washington, DC: National Council of Architectural Registration Boards, 2014. http://www.ncarb.org/About-NCARB/~/media/Files/PDF/Special-Paper/NCARB_by_the _Numbers_2014.ashx.

New York Times. "Women Architects Win Chicago Prize: Best Plans for a Neighborhood." March 6, 1915.

———. "Women Gain Slowly in Technical Fields." January 17, 1949.

New York Tribune. "Planned by Two Women: Model Tenement-Houses to Be Built Soon in This City." February 24, 1895.

O'Hare, Marita. "Foreword." In *Women in American Architecture: A Historic and Contemporary Perspective*, ed. Susana Torre, 6–7. New York: Whitney Library of Design, 1977.

Olcayto, Rory. "Discrimination Starts in the Studio." *Architects' Journal*, January 23, 2015. http://www.architectsjournal.co.uk/discrimination-starts-in-the-studio /8676381.article.

———. "Pritzker Prize: Denise Scott Brown Should Have Won in '91." *Architects' Journal*, March 19, 2013.

Oldershaw, Barbara. "Developing a Feminist Critique of Architecture." *Gender and Design*. Special issue, *Design Book Review* 25 (Summer 1992): 7–15.

One Fine Day. Directed by Michael Hoffman, 1996. Los Angeles, CA: 20th Century Fox, 2003. DVD.

Orenstein, Peggy. *Cinderella Ate My Daughter: Dispatches from the Front Lines of the New Girlie-Girl Culture*. New York: HarperCollins, 2011.

Otten, Liam, "Women in Architecture." Washington University in St. Louis Newsroom, October 31, 2014. https://news.wustl.edu/news/Pages/27622.aspx.

Ouroussoff, Nicolai. "First Woman Wins Pritzker." *Los Angeles Times*, March 22, 2004.

Paine, Judith. "Pioneer Women Architects." In *Women in American Architecture: A Historic and Contemporary Perspective*, ed. Susana Torre, 54–69. New York: Whitney Library of Design, 1977.

Pogrebin, Robin. "Partner without the Prize." *New York Times*, April 17, 2013.

———. "Pritzker Architecture Prize Goes to Shigeru Ban." *New York Times*, March 24, 2014.

Poore, Nancy. "Woman Architect Cashes in on Design Talent." *Chicago Tribune*, March 13, 1966.

Potter, Claire. "Prikipedia? Or, Looking for the Women on Wikipedia." *Chronicle of Higher Education*, March 10, 2013. http://chronicle.com/blognetwork/tenuredradical.

Pritzker Architecture Prize. "Architect Robert Venturi Is Named the 1991 Pritzker Architecture Prize Laureate." http://www.pritzkerprize.com/1991/announcement.

———. "Architectural Partners in Japan Become the 2010 Pritzker Architecture Prize Laureates." http://www.pritzkerprize.com/2010/announcement.

Proceedings of the West Coast Women's Design Conference, April 18–20, 1974, University of Oregon. N.p.: West Coast Women's Design Conference, 1975.

Quindlen, Anna. "Barbie at 35." In *The Barbie Chronicles: A Living Doll Turns Forty*, ed. Yona Zeldis McDonough, 117–19. New York: Touchstone, 1999.

Rand, Ayn. *The Fountainhead*. New York: Signet, 1993.

Reif, Rita. "Fighting the System in the Male-Dominated Field of Architecture." *New York Times*, April 11, 1971.

———. "Women Architects, Slow to Unite, Find They're Catching Up with Male Peers." *New York Times*, February 26, 1973.

Rendell, Jane, Barbara Penner, and Iain Borden. *Gender, Space, Architecture: An*

Interdisciplinary Introduction. London: Routledge, 2000.

Richardson, Anne. "Half the Mothers I Know Have Been Driven from Their Jobs." *Guardian*, August 8, 2013. http://www.theguardian.com/money/2013/aug/08 /workplace-discrimination-pregnant-women-mothers-common.

Ridge, Mia. "New Challenges in Digital History: Sharing Women's History on Wikipedia." Paper delivered at the Women's History in the Digital World Conference, Bryn Mawr College, Bryn Mawr, PA, March 23, 2013. http://repository.brynmawr .edu/greenfield_conference/papers/saturday/37.

Roehrig, Catharine H., Renée Dreyfus, and Cathleen A. Keller, eds. *Hatshepsut, From Queen to Pharaoh*. New York: Metropolitan Museum of Art, and New Haven, CT: Yale University Press, 2005.

Rosenfield, Karissa. "Shereen Sherzad Wins the 2014 Tamayouz Women in Architecture and Construction Award." *ArchDaily*, November 4, 2014. http://www .archdaily.com/?p=563900.

Rüedi, Katerina, Sarah Wigglesworth, and Duncan McCorquodale, eds. *Desiring Practices: Architecture, Gender and the Interdisciplinary*. London: Black Dog, 1996.

Saint, Andrew. *The Image of the Architect*. New Haven, CT: Yale University Press, 1983.

Sandberg, Sheryl. *Lean In: Women, Work, and the Will to Lead*. New York: Knopf, 2013.

Sanders, James. "Robert Venturi: Denise Scott Brown: An Architectural Team to Reshape the American Landscape." *Los Angeles Times*, August 18, 1991.

Sanders, Joel, ed. *Stud: Architectures of Masculinity*. New York: Princeton Architectural Press, 1996.

Scheffler, Karl. *Die Frau und die Kunst* [Woman and art]. Berlin: Julius Bard, 1908.

——— . "Vom Beruf und von den Aufgaben des modernen Architekten" [On the profession and responsibilities of the modern architect]. 2 parts. *Süddeutsche Bauzeitung* 19, no. 13 (1909): 97–103, and no. 14, 106–10.

Schmidt, Peter. "Michigan Overwhelmingly Adopts Ban on Affirmative-Action Preferences." *Chronicle of Higher Education*, November 17, 2006, A23–A24.

Schriener, Judy. "Architect Barbie in the Offing?" *Construction*, December 5, 2002. http://www.construction.com/NewsCenter/it/archive/20021205apf.asp. Site no longer working.

Scott Brown, Denise. "Room at the Top: Sexism and the Star System in Architecture." In *Architecture: A Place for Women*, ed. Ellen Perry Berkeley and Matilda McQuaid, 237–46. Washington, DC: Smithsonian Institution Press, 1989.

——— . "Sexism and the Star System in Architecture: A Lecture by Denise Scott Brown." Synopsis published in *Proceedings of the West Coast Women's Design Conference, April 18–20, 1974, University of Oregon*. N.p.: West Coast Women's Design Conference, 1975, 20–21.

Searing, Helen, et al. "Equal and Unequal Partners, 1881–1970." In *Equal Partners: Men and Women Principals in Contemporary Architectural Practice*. Northampton, MA: Smith College Museum of Art, 1998, 22–39.

——— . *Equal Partners: Men and Women Principals in Contemporary Architectural Practice*. Northampton, MA: Smith College Museum of Art, 1998.

Shen, Aviva. "How Many Women Does It Take to Change Wikipedia?" *Smithsonian*, April 4, 2012. http://www.smithsonianmag.com/smithsonian-institution/how -many-women-does-it-take-to-change-wikipedia-171400755/?no-ist=.

Sheng, Rosa. "Equity by Design: AtlAlAnta! Convention Recap." *Equity by Design: Missing 32 Percent Blog*, May 17, 2015. http://themissing32percent.com/blog/2015 /5/17/equity-by-design-aia-convention-atlanta-recap.

Sieder, Jill Jordan. "A Building of Her Own." *U.S. News and World Report*, October 14, 1996, 66–68.

Simon, Cathy. "Women in Architecture: What Are We Doing Here?" *Contract* 45, no. 3 (2003): 94.

Sparke, Penny. *As Long as It's Pink: The Sexual Politics of Taste*. London: HarperCollins, 1995.

Storefront for Art and Architecture. "Wwwriting Series: Digital Invisibles." http://www.storefrontnews.org/archive/2010?y=0&m=0&p=0&c=10&e=616.

Stratigakos, Despina. "Architects in Skirts: The Public Image of Women Architects in Wilhelmine Germany." *Journal of Architectural Education* 55, no. 2 (2001): 90–100.

———. "The Good Architect and the Bad Parent: On the Formation and Disruption of a Canonical Image." *Journal of Architecture* 13, no. 3 (2008): 283–96.

———. "'I Myself Want to Build': Women, Architectural Education and the Integration of Germany's Technical Colleges." *Paedagogica Historica* 43, no. 6 (2007): 727–56.

———. "The Uncanny Architect: Fears of Lesbian Builders and Deviant Homes in Modern Germany." In *Negotiating Domesticity: Spatial Productions of Gender in Modern Architecture*, ed. Hilde Heynen and Gülsüm Baydar, 145–61. London: Routledge, 2005.

———. "Unforgetting Women Architects: From Pritzker to Wikipedia." *Places Journal*, June 2013. http://places.designobserver.com/feature/unforgetting-women-architects-from-pritzker-to-wikipedia/37912.

———. "What I Learned from Architect Barbie," *Places Journal*, June 2011, http://places.designobserver.com/feature/what-i-learned-from-architect-barbie/27638.

———. "Women and the Werkbund: Gender Politics and German Design Reform, 1907–14." *Journal of the Society of Architectural Historians* 62, no. 4 (2003): 490–511.

———. *A Women's Berlin*. Minneapolis: University of Minnesota Press, 2008.

Sun (Baltimore). "Closet Wonders." June 11, 1911.

Suominen-Kokkonen, Renja. *The Fringe of a Profession: Women as Architects in Finland from the 1890s to the 1950s*. Trans. Jüri Kokkonen. Helsinki, 1992.

Times Pictorial (*Irish Times*). "Women Should Design Houses." February 21, 1953.

Torre, Susana. "Introduction: A Parallel History." In *Women in American Architecture: A Historic and Contemporary Perspective*, ed. Susana Torre, 10–13. New York: Whitney Library of Design, 1977.

———. "Women in Architecture and the New Feminism." In *Women in American Architecture: A Historic and Contemporary Perspective*, ed. Susana Torre, 148–61. New York: Whitney Library of Design, 1977.

———, ed. *Women in American Architecture: A Historic and Contemporary Perspective*. New York: Whitney Library of Design, 1977.

Tracings: A Newsletter of the Environmental Design Archives. "Down the Rabbit Hole: (Miss)Adventures in Wikipedia." Vol. 11, no. 1 (2015).

Troiani, Igea. "Zaha: An Image of 'The Woman Architect.'" Women, Practice, Architecture. Special issue, *Architectural Theory Review* 17, nos. 2–3 (2012): 346–64.

U.S. Bureau of Labor Statistics. "Household Data Annual Averages," 2014. http://www.bls.gov/cps/cpsaat39.pdf.

Van Slyck, Abigail A. "Women in Architecture and the Problems of Biography." *Gender and Design*. Special issue, *Design Book Review* 25 (Summer 1992): 19–22.

Wainwright, Oliver. "Zaha Hadid's Sport Stadiums: 'Too Big, Too Expensive, Too Much Like a Vagina.'" *Guardian*, November 28, 2013. http://www.theguardian.com/artanddesign/2013/nov/28/zaha-hadid-stadiums-vagina.

Waite, Richard. "Call for Denise Scott Brown to Be Given Pritzker Recognition." *Architects' Journal*, March 21, 2013.

———. "Video Exclusive: Denise Scott Brown on Why She Deserves Pritzker Recognition." *Architects' Journal*, April 10, 2013. http://www.architectsjournal.co.uk/video-exclusive-denise-scott-brown-on-why-she-deserves-pritzker-recognition/8645333.article.

————. "'Women Need to Support Each Other,' Says Zaha after Winning Jane Drew Prize." *Architects' Journal*, April 20, 2012. http://www.architectsjournal.co.uk/news /daily-news/women-need-to-support-each-other-says-zaha-after-winning-jane -drew-prize/8629310.article.

Waite, Richard, and Ann-Marie Corvin. "Shock Survey Results as the AJ Launches Campaign to Raise Women Architects' Status." *Architects' Journal*, January 16, 2012. http://www.architectsjournal.co.uk/news/daily-news/shock-survey-results -as-the-aj-launches-campaign-to-raise-women-architects-status/8624748.article.

Walker, Alissa. "Architecture Is Tough! Will Architect Barbie Help More Women Become Designers?" *Good.is*, March 3, 2011. http://magazine.good.is/articles/architecture -is-tough-will-architect-barbie-help-more-women-become-designers.

Walker, Lynne. "Women Architects." In *A View From the Interior: Women and Design*, ed. Judy Attfield and Pat Kirkham, 90–105. London: Women's Press, 1995.

Washington Post. "The Woman Architect." September 26, 1880.

Watson, Stephen T. "Professor Builds Case for Barbie as Architect." *Buffalo News*, February 7, 2010.

Weimann, Jeanne Madeline. *The Fair Women*. Chicago: Academy Chicago, 1981.

Weisman, Leslie Kanes. *Discrimination by Design: A Feminist Critique of the Man-Made Environment*. Urbana: University of Illinois Press, 1992.

————. "A Feminist Experiment: Learning from WSPA, Then and Now." In *Architecture: A Place for Women*, ed. Ellen Perry Berkeley and Matilda McQuaid, 125–33. Washington, DC: Smithsonian Institution Press, 1989.

Weisman, Leslie Kanes, and Noel Phyllis Birkby. "The Women's School of Planning and Architecture." In *Learning Our Way: Essays in Feminist Education*, ed. Charlotte Bunch and Sandra Pollack, 224–45. Trumansburg, NY: Crossing Press, 1983.

Willis, Beverly. "The Lone Heroic Architect Is Passé." Opinion pages, *New York Times*, July 15, 2014. http://www.nytimes.com/roomfordebate/2013/05/14/married-to-an -award winner/the-lone-heroic-architect-is-passe.

Willis, Eric. "Five Firm Changes." *Architect*, October 2014, 116–24.

Willis, Julie, and Bronwyn Hanna. *Women Architects in Australia, 1900–1950*. Red Hill, Australia: Royal Australian Institute of Architects, 2001.

Winston, Anna. "Mattel Reveals Architect Barbie." *BDonline*, February 21, 2011. http:// www.bdonline.co.uk/mattel-reveals-architect-barbie/5013092.article.

————. "The Top 10 News Stories of 2011." *BDonline*, December 30, 2011. http://www .bdonline.co.uk/the-top-10-news-stories-of-2011/5029650.article.

Woodward, Helen. "The Woman Who Makes Good: Women as Architects." *Chicago Defender*, June 10, 1933.

Wright, Gwendolyn. "On the Fringe of the Profession: Women in American Architecture." In *The Architect: Chapters in the History of the Profession*, ed. Spiro Kostof, 280–308. New York: Oxford University Press, 1977.

Index

Filipacchi, Amanda, 73–74, 75
Financial Times, 52
Freedman, Nina, 25
French Royal Academy of Architecture, 60
Fuller, Buckminster, 77

Gang, Jeanne, 74
Gannon, Mary, 12
Gardner, Sue, 69, 76
gender: categorization of women
    and minorities, on Wikipedia,
    73–75; concepts of femininity and
    architecture, 5–9, 10–12, 13–14, 15,
    40, 42; Hadid's winning of Pritzker
    Prize, gender-based response to,
    50–54; hypermasculinity viewed as
    desirable architectural quality, 8–9,
    11, 12; monograph format, biases of,
    66; style judgments, gender-based,
    9–12; "Women in Architecture"
    surveys, male versus female
    responses, 81–82
gender discrimination: in architecture
    schools, 21–26; current women
    architects experiencing, 28, 30, 31–34,
    80; historical experience of, 33; salary
    gap, 28, 33, 34, 43, 80–82
generational differences in perception of
    Architect Barbie, 44–47
Glasgow, Riverside Museum, *51*
Gleick, James, 74
Google and Googling, 71–73
Gray, Eileen, 74
Greece, women architects in, 35
Griffin, Marion Mahony, 74
Griffiths, Diana, 30
Groat, Linda N., 86–87n13
GRoW Home, *81*
Guardian, 42, 50–52
Guerilla Girls, 40

Hadid, Zaha, 3, 23, 50–54, *51*, 55, 56, 61,
    63–64, 80
Hands, Alice, 12
Harvard Graduate School of Design, 3,
    56, *58*
Hatshepsut, 65
Hayden, Sophia, 10, 11–12
Heathcote, Edwin, 52
Herzog, Jacques, 54
Hickey, Patricia, 32
Hicks, Margaret, 6
historical background (1870s–1970s),

1, 5–20; concepts of femininity and
    architecture, 5–9, 13–14, 15; domestic
    architecture, association of women
    with, 6, 9–10, 13–14, 83n4; gender
    discrimination experienced by women
    architects, 33; gender-based style
    judgments, 9–12; hypermasculinity
    viewed as desirable architectural
    quality, 8–9, 11, 12; prizes and awards,
    12–13, 60; suffragists, 6; women
    as percentage of architects in U.S.
    (1926-1975), 15; women's liberation
    movement (1960s–1970s), 14–19;
    worlds' fairs and exhibitions, women's
    pavilions at, 10–12; writings about
    women architects, 1970s increase in,
    18–19, 23; WWII housing boom, 13–14
historical writings about women architects.
    See writings about women architects
Howe, Julia Ward, 5–6
Huxtable, Ada Louise, 14–15, 19
Hyatt Foundation, 60, 67

Illinois Institute of Technology, 48
Indesign, 43
International Archive of Women in Archi-
    tecture, Blacksburg, Virginia, 65–66
Internet: online presence, importance of
    women architects', 3–4, 68–69, 71–73;
    Wikipedia, 3–4, 69–76, 77–79
Italcementi Group, Italy, 63
Ivy, Robert, 53–54

James, Caroline, 56, *58*, 58–59, 75
Jane Drew Prize, *Architects' Journal*,
    62, 63
Jeffries, Stuart, 50–52
Jensen, Julia, 40
Jezebel, 43

Karlsruhe Institute of Technology, 69
Kay, Jane Holtz, 16
Kellog, Fay, 10, 13
Kiran Curtis Associates, 34
Knüppelholz-Roeser, Margarete, 10–11
Koolhaas, Rem, 56

Lacy, Bill, 61–62
Lange, Alexandra, 61
lawyers, female, 35–36
Lee, Amy, 42
Leipzig International Book Fair (1913), 10
Letters to the Mayor (Storefront for Art

Photo Credits

1. "Ein weiblicher Maurergeselle," *Die Frau im Osten* 6, no. 15 (1912): 115.
2. "Frauen als Baumeister," *Illustrierte Frauenzeitung* 38, no. 2 (1910): 17.
3. Organization of Women Architects. Photo by Jeremiah Bragstad.
4. © AIASF, all rights reserved.
5. Courtesy of Mattel, Inc.
6. Courtesy of Despina Stratigakos. Photo by Paige Hammerschmidt and Caryn Schadegg.
7. Courtesy of Mattel, Inc.
8. Jeff J. Mitchell, Getty Images News, Getty Images.
9. Change.org.
10. Photography by Bryce Vickmark, Boston.
11. Courtesy of Wikimedia Commons.
12. Courtesy of Werner Firgau.
13. Courtesy of Storefront for Art and Architecture.
14. Courtesy of Megan Basnak.
15. Photograph by Zhi Ting, courtesy of the University at Buffalo School of Architecture and Planning.

Places Books is published by Princeton University Press in association with *Places Journal*. Founded in 1983, *Places Journal* is dedicated to harnessing the moral and investigative power of public scholarship to promote equitable cities and sustainable landscapes. The journal is supported by an international network of academic partners whose collective generosity made possible the original essays, "What I Learned from Architect Barbie" and "Unforgetting Women Architects," which are the bases for this volume of Places Books.

Places' partner network comprises the Aarhus School of Architecture, École Polytechnique Fédérale de Lausanne, ETH Zürich, Georgia Institute of Technology, Lund University, Massachusetts Institute of Technology, Pratt Institute, SCI-Arc, Tulane University, University of British Columbia, University of California at Berkeley, University of Hong Kong, University of Manitoba, University of Miami, University of Michigan, University of Pennsylvania, University of Southern California, University of Texas at Austin, University of Toronto, University of Virginia, University of Washington, and Woodbury University.

placesjournal.org